Grandma Doralee Patinkin's Holiday Cookbook

A Jewish Family's Celebrations

Also by Doralee Patinkin Rubin

⚘ ⚘ ⚘

Grandma Doralee Patinkin's
Jewish Family Cookbook

Grandma Doralee Patinkin's Holiday Cookbook

A Jewish Family's Celebrations

Doralee Patinkin Rubin

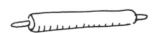

ST. MARTIN'S PRESS NEW YORK

Design and illustration by Jill Weber

Library of Congress Cataloging-in-Publication Data

Rubin, Doralee Patinkin.
Grandma Doralee Patinkin's holiday cookbook :
a Jewish family's celebrations / Doralee Patinkin Rubin.
p.   cm.
Includes index.
ISBN 0-312-24196-8
1. Cookery, Jewish.   2. Holiday cookery.   I. Title.
TX724.R655   1999   99-15929
641.5'676–dc21   CIP

First Edition: October 1999

10   9   8   7   6   5   4   3   2   1

This book is dedicated to all my loving family
and friends who over the years graced my table.
Without their appreciation of my efforts,
I would not be who I am.

In Memory

of all my dear and departed
who guided me through the years
and taught me so much.

Contents

Preface

Dear Friends,

Having written my first book and realizing I still had so much to say, I thought it might be helpful if I shared with you some of my thoughts on holiday entertaining.

Holidays were always a festive time for the family and, of course, food was of paramount importance. Sometimes we had sit-down dinners, sometimes buffets—a football game, a bridal luncheon, a holiday, or a brunch, I always tried to keep it simple and delicious.

In this book I suggest menus for various occasions. A few of the more traditional recipes may have appeared in my first cookbook, *Grandma Doralee Patinkin's Jewish Family Cookbook*, but it is appropriate that they appear once again. Keep in mind, these are only suggestions.

I could not possibly have entertained all these years without the input of my children, friends, and extended family. I am most grateful for their help and suggestions and for the recipes given to me over the years.

I recently had the pleasure of meeting Joan Nathan, author of *Jewish Cooking in America*. In reading her scholarly work, I realized that many of my recipes, which I have prepared for more than fifty years, are, in reality, over one hundred years old. Jewish cooking in America has survived with a little change here and there, and I am confident that some of these recipes will be around for many generations to come.

There are certain foods that define certain holidays, such as potato latkes on Hanukkah and Hamentashen at Purim, but most traditional meals can be drawn from the rich lore of Jewish cooking. The types of foods may vary considerably because of the dispersion of our people all over the world. As Jews settled in a country, they would adopt some of the cuisine indigenous to that land, and it became part of the Jewish food heritage. Wherever Jews settled, they eventually began to adopt the customs and rituals of that land as well as many of the flavors of their foods.

That is why there are so many versions of traditional foods, and they are all correct.

While this is not a kosher cookbook, almost any recipe can be adapted for a kosher table if it is important to you. I hope that by making the necessary changes, you will find that you, too, can be a wonderful Jewish cook.

If you find that I have omitted certain traditional foods, such as challah, knishes, and Hamentashen, it is because I never made them. I always found a marvelous Jewish bakery and availed myself of their wares. If I didn't prepare a traditional dish, it does not belong in "my" book.

Food is bound up in our memories of all our holidays as it is in any ethnic origin. We all have fond memories of holidays celebrated with friends and family, and they usually include some specific food.

While our family always prepared latkes (or anything fried in oil) as symbolic food for Hanukkah, it has recently come to my attention that there is a seldom-told story about celebrating the holiday by eating cheesecake. It is found in the Book of Judith. I checked the authenticity of this tale with my stepson, Rabbi Robert Rubin, and he said it is a tale seldom told because the Book of Judith came so much later in our history. The cheesecake symbolizes the cheeses that Judith fed the Assyrian general Holofernes, who was about to attack the Jewish people. He became very thirsty; she plied him with wine, and he fell asleep. She then proceeded to cut off his head, thus freeing her people from the Assyrians.

As cheesecake has always been my favorite dessert, I was delighted to hear this story. In the future, a cheesecake will always appear on my table during Hanukkah.

Entertaining, for me, has always been fun; I would like you to have the same experience. I have tried to present these recipes as simply as possible, so decide what you like, relax, and enjoy your guests.

Daralee Patinkin Rubin

Special Thanks

To Kathryn and Mandy, who have been with me every step of the way, for believing in me and my ability to become an author. You light up my life.

To the rest of my family: Stanley, Marsha Patinkin Schwartzman and George Schwartzman, Joanne and Ken Gimbel, Bonnie and Neal Rubin, Patty and Alan Rubin, Susan and Bob Rubin, and all my grandchildren. Thank you for your love and encouragement.

To Joan Nathan and Edie Greenberg, eminent authors in their own right. Thank you so much for the recognition given me.

And last but not least, to my editor, Marian Lizzi, and the entire staff at St. Martin's Press. It has been a pleasure being associated with you.

Grandma Doralee Patinkin's Holiday Cookbook

A Jewish Family's Celebrations

Introduction

BY Mandy Patinkin

When it comes to a party or holiday spread, nobody beats my ma.

Rosh Hashanah, Yom Kippur, Thanksgiving, Hanukkah, Passover, birthdays, bar/bat mitzvahs, you name it, my ma laid out the best spread in the world.

The four greatest things I've ever done in my life were marrying my wife, Kathryn, having my two children, Isaac and Gideon, and asking my ma to write down her recipes for all her grandchildren, and yours truly. So if you are reading this it will make you one of my ma's grandchildren. Welcome to the family!

As a kid, I remember the holidays starting with a new coat of wax on the floor and, sure enough, I'd come running into the house and lay down a brand new set of skid marks.

Once she recovered from this ritual, she proceeded to instruct me not to touch the dessert trays that were laden with powdered sugar cookies and the best brownies in the world. I always managed to find a way to steal a few when she wasn't looking, and rearrange the trays (in a genetically inherited fashion).

The house was immaculate and the tables were beautifully set. All I hoped for then, as I do today, was my fair share of my ma's hot cream cheese and hot mushroom hors d'oeuvres. By the time I devoured half of what she made, I never had room for the brisket.

Whether we were twisting the crepe paper streamers for Hanukkah or birthday parties, which sometimes fell during Hanukkah, making sure there were plenty of pennies for the game of dreydel, making the charoses for Passover or the latkes for Hanukkah, stuffing the turkey, arranging the Fannie May candies in the trays, always looking for the chocolate creams (a gift my grandma Celia seemed to have down pat), Mom included the entire family in the preparation. That was the key to the whole ballgame—she knew each event was a family affair and she wasn't about to have it any other way.

Without a doubt, the key jobs were to lick the cake or brownie bowl (long before we learned of the dangers of raw eggs), put powdered sugar on the brownies or butter balls, put up the decorations, or try to taste the chocolate matzo before the company came.

Nothing was more fun than trying to figure out all the possible options for hiding the "affikomin." The year that stumped all of us was when my dad (he wore those long black socks that came up all the way to the knee) shoved the affikomin inside his sock and then secured it with tape. I cannot remember who found it, but I know it wasn't me. The hitch that year was that when we went to compare the two halves of the affikomin, we discovered that Grandma Celia had eaten the other half. Never fear, the winner was awarded anyway.

Holiday memories are the golden days of my childhood. I longed for them and was terrified of them at the same time. You see, I loved the food and the games and the celebrations, but I was terrified of a few of my older cousins who took great pleasure in tormenting me. Truth be told, in at least fifty percent of the instances I'm sure I brought it on myself, but as for the other fifty percent, I still plead "not guilty."

To this day, our family parties are beautiful. The brunches are glorious, and the tables always look as though they could feed a small country. Mom never arrives for an out-of-town occasion, or for that matter just a simple visit, empty-handed. She always comes with a spare suitcase filled with home-baked goodies, and that starts the engine of that famous phrase for the next two weeks, "I'm starting my diet as soon as Grandma Doralee's butter cookies are gone."

Please try some of my ma's holiday treats and share some of my memories.

MANDY PATINKIN

Introductions from My Family Table

THERE IS ONLY ONE REASON *I dread my mother-in-law coming to town—it means I will seriously gain at least ten pounds. I usually beg her not to bring the butter cookies, but she knows I don't really mean it. I not only enjoy the way they melt at the moment, but the taste sensation is so tremendous that I can literally savor them months later.*

🌹 Kathryn Grody

FOR ALMOST FIFTY YEARS, *I have been a disciple in my mother's kitchen. Mom serves up a rich confection: a culinary esperanto laced with a sense of dynastic pride. Her cooking fills so much more than my recipe box.*

Blending the traditional and the experimental, she understands the imperatives to take risks, to strategize, to organize, to produce, to critique, to revise, and then begin anew.

Ever-focused on superior cuisine and gracious hospitality, she is engaged in an intricate process whose elements guarantee delicious meals and successful entertaining. As my husband, George Schwartzman, says, she presides, and does that so very well.

Her cookbooks are veritable treasure troves of edible masterpieces that will dazzle everyone's grand "mishpacha" (extended family).

🌹 Marsha Patinkin Schwartzman

There's Yellowstone, Niagara Falls, *the Grand Tetons, and Everest, but none of them compare to the height and majesty of my grandma's baked buffets. The smells and tastes of her kitchen have laced my childhood since the beginning of my memories. I hope that this book will enable other children to experience a piece of my grandma's true gift.*

🌹 Isaac Grody Patinkin

I'm exhausted. *My family always does everything at the last minute. It drives me nuts. This is what I have to say about my grandma's brownies and potato latkes: "I'm going off to dream about them right this second, and they are going to be fantastic dreams."*

🌹 Gideon Grody Patinkin

For more than twenty-five years *I've felt blessed to have Doris, not only as a wonderful grandma for my three daughters and as a very gracious, wise, helpful, and fun mother-in-law, but also as a resource par excellence for cooking and entertaining.*

What stands out in my mind as my most favorite recipes? Well, her little butter crisps are the absolute tops! But those miniature strudels, her mandelbrot, and her toffee squares are close seconds. Her carrot pudding is truly legendary. So is her fruit compote. And I've gotten a lot of mileage out of her chocolate-dipped apricots. Truly, the list goes on and on.

Doris is the one who introduced me to the indispensable nature of both the food processor and the microwave. I resisted both those "new inventions" for a very long time. But she persevered, and then finally she actually gave them to me as gifts. And she was sooo right—within a few weeks, I couldn't live without them.

She also introduced me to the pleasures of sun-dried tomatoes, the tastiness of smoked turkey, the beauty of presenting desserts on different tiers, and the lovely presentation made by setting up a buffet using wicker baskets for display. There have been all kinds of other culinary tricks I have learned from Doris, and lots of hints for more healthful eating as well.

I believe that the three key ingredients in all her culinary creations are simplicity, attractiveness, and delicious taste. It's always clear how much enjoyment and fulfillment she gets from being in the kitchen. That alone is a great model for all of us. In Doris's hands, cooking, baking, and entertaining is really an art as well as an expression of caring. She definitely epitomizes the commercial jingle "nothin' says lovin' like somethin' from the oven."

 Bonnie Rubin

THE ABILITY TO COOK IS, *unfortunately, not hereditary. The phrase "salt and pepper to taste" has always baffled me, and I haven't yet fully mastered the art of sautéeing. I have, however, learned over the years the importance of family and tradition. I have an enormous extended family and when we come together for various occasions, food always seems to be at the center of the event.*

No Thanksgiving would be the same without my grandma's homemade cranberry sauce, and a bar mitzvah simply could not take place minus thousands of toffee bars. As a little girl, I remember watching my grandma bake for hours, and now, as an adult, I call her often with cooking questions, or in a panic when I can't decide what appetizer I should take to a dinner party. I am extremely grateful that my grandma has taken the time to compile her recipes, so that when I finally conquer the kitchen, I can continue the family traditions with my children and their children.

Thank you, Grandma, for your wonderful cookbooks and years of inspiration.

 Lainie Rubenstein

GOING TO GRANDMA AND GRANDPA'S HOUSE *in Hyde Park was always such a treat for me. Not only was I intrigued by the beautiful chandeliers, which I was sure were made out of diamonds, but I was also lured by Grandma's buffet table, which was always laden with my favorite foods. I would fill my plate with orange marmalade soufflé, which I just couldn't get enough of, cheese blintzes with blueberries on top, noodle kugel that no one can top, and always still have room for Grandma's signature dish—brownies with chocolate jimmies on top. (To this day, no one can make them like she can!)*

After the wonderfully endless meal came the third thing I loved about visiting Grandma and Grandpa—our dance performance. Needless to say, Grandma and Grandpa were our best audience, cheering wildly at every spin, leap, and wobble my sisters and I made. I could only hope that she'd let us do it all again the next Sunday.

Although I may never have diamondlike chandeliers in my own house, I do hope one day to share with my own children the delicious treats made with such love and care that added so sweetly to the memories of my childhood.

 Karie Rubin

OVER THE YEARS, *my grandmother has made me butter crisps, cream cheese brownies, apple-raisin strudel, carrot pudding, blintz soufflé, spinach lasagne, carrot salad, gazpacho mold, ambrosia, and various other yummy treats.*

Being 1,000 miles away, it's a little tough for my grandmother to feed me. Therefore, I have taught Adam, my husband, how to cook.

But, it's just not the same.

I love you!

Love always,

    ❀ Laurie Rubin Glaser

I REMEMBER WHEN I WAS A LITTLE GIRL *my Grandma Doralee came to stay with us when my parents were out of town. Of course, I was so excited because I knew we would be having some special treats. My grandma invents whatever recipe she wants, but her butter crisps will always be my absolute favorite. When her stay with us came to an end, my grandma left, especially for me, ten rolls of frozen butter crisps so that I could make my own after she left.*

Thank you, Grandma, for creating such wonderful memories for all of your grandchildren.

    ❀ Amanda Patinkin

WHAT STANDS OUT IN MY MIND *about the countless meals served at my grandparents' homes in Chicago while I was growing up is the buffet table.*

Whether we were feasting on Grandma Doralee's homemade goodies (she always made it look so easy!) or just ordering in from Carson's for ribs, the food was always so beautifully presented on platters and laid out on the buffet.

And the desserts! After devouring samplings of kuchens or perhaps brownies or mandelbrot, the group would all retire to the living room where we grandchildren would put on a dance performance to whatever music was on hand, as the grown-ups "oohed" and "aahed" accordingly.

Ever after Grandma and Grandpa moved to San Diego, and we grandchildren began to think we were "too cool" to spontaneously prance around the living room in our stocking feet, the tradition of Grandma's wonderful recipes continued to be a staple at all of our holiday and family meals. We repeatedly enjoyed not just carrot pudding, but GRANDMA'S carrot pudding, GRANDMA'S blintz soufflé, GRANDMA'S brisket, GRANDMA'S mini cheesecakes, Doris's recipe for BUTTER CRISPS. The dish would rise to a new level of eminence with this coveted title!

Over the years, I have come to associate those familiar dishes and flavors and smells with family and with fond memories and tradition. Grandma's cooking is nourishment for the palate as well as the soul.

As an adult, I now have my own kitchen. When I entertain, prepare a seder meal, make Hanukkah latkes, cookies, etc., I immediately go for Grandma's recipes, because for me, the meal and the experience is not complete without them.

Thanks, Gram, for putting them all in a book so that now I have "Grandma's special recipes" at my fingertips in the kitchen, and I'm forever saved from the frantic last-minute phone calls to my mom or to you!

 Debra Rubin

GRANDMA,

I admire all the hard work you have put into this book, and as I told you at my bar mitzvah, I'll be sure to eat my share.

With much love,

Your grandson,

🌹 Leslie Rubenstein

WE CAN EASILY REMEMBER THE SHOE BOXES *of yummy baked goods shipped straight to our door from Grandma's kitchen in time for our bar mitzvahs. From chocolate chip–peanut butter cups to almond bars and miniature cheese-cakes, Grandma's sweet table was always a wonder to behold and a joy to eat.*

Thanks, Grandma, for the delicious food and wonderful memories!

🌹 David and Matthew Rubin

WHEN I WAS VERY YOUNG, *Hanukkah always meant family, gifts, vacation, and making latkes with Grandma Doralee. I remember piling all of my mini kitchenware into the car and shlepping it to Grandma's kitchen counter, where it would sit while I used real potato peelers and real bowls to make the infa-mous pancakes.*

Grandma always made the best latkes around. Afterward, we'd take a break at the local miniature golf park, where we'd enjoy the San Diego sun in the middle of December.

🌹 Becky Gimbel

𝒥T'S ALWAYS INTERESTING *going over to Grandma's house. I don't think I've* *ever gone over there and had the same thing to eat twice. Whether it be the* *food, or the conversation, it's always fun when I'm at my grandparents' house.* *Whenever we have family in from out of town, we always meet them at* *Grandma's. Let the secret be known—they come for the food, and for me.*

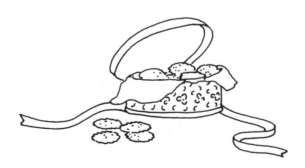

Jeremy Gimbel

Rosh Hashanah

Rosh Hashanah

The first day of Rosh Hashanah was and still is a very festive time for my entire family. We are now fragmented, some in the East, some in the Midwest, and the rest of us now in the West; but, whether we gather together or separately, we rejoice in welcoming the Jewish New Year, first in prayer in our temples and then, where else but around the table enjoying a beautiful holiday meal.

It is traditional to begin with apples dipped in honey, thanking God for the fruit of the earth and hoping for a sweet year ahead for everyone.

May your holiday be sweet, may the next year be a healthy one, and may the New Year bring peace to all.

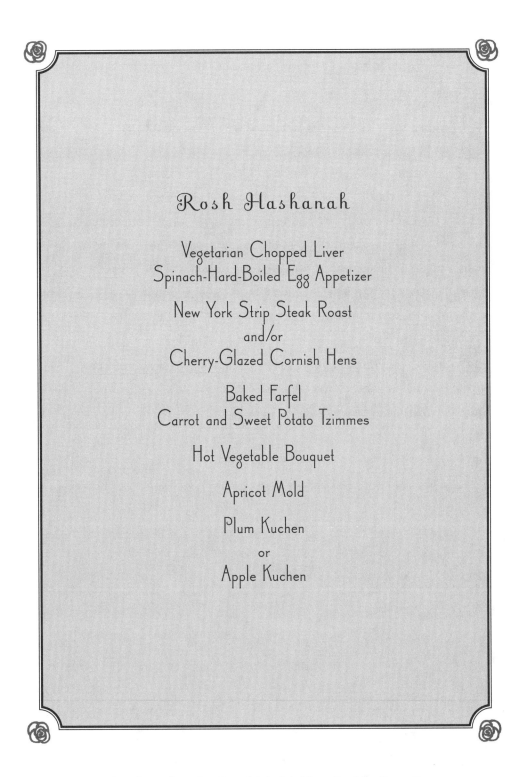

Rosh Hashanah

Vegetarian Chopped Liver
Spinach-Hard-Boiled Egg Appetizer

New York Strip Steak Roast
and/or
Cherry-Glazed Cornish Hens

Baked Farfel
Carrot and Sweet Potato Tzimmes

Hot Vegetable Bouquet

Apricot Mold

Plum Kuchen
or
Apple Kuchen

Vegetarian Chopped Liver

A wonderful substitute for the real thing. Joan Nathan was kind enough to feature me on one of her PBS segments of "Jewish Cooking in America," preparing this in Mandy and Kathryn's kitchen in Manhattan.

In a deep frying pan, heat the peanut oil. Add the sliced onions and sauté for at least 1 hour. Place all the ingredients in a food processor and process until smooth. Do not overprocess. Place in refrigerator for several hours. Serve with cocktail rye or crackers or place some filling on an endive leaf and garnish with a strip of the red bell pepper.

YIELD: 6 TO 8 SERVINGS

¼ cup peanut oil

4 large onions, sliced

2 cups canned string beans, drained

½ cup canned peas, drained

4 whites of hard-boiled eggs (optional)

½ cup walnuts

salt and pepper to taste

Belgian endive and red bell pepper cut into strips or cocktail rye or crackers

Spinach—Hard-Boiled-Egg Appetizer

This is a delicious vegetarian appetizer. It is especially nice for those who observe the dietary restrictions. It makes a firm mold, or you can serve it in a beautiful bowl.

1	10-ounce package frozen chopped spinach, cooked and drained
1	sweet onion, finely diced
8	hard-boiled eggs, finely chopped (whites only if so desired)
1	tablespoon mayonnaise
⅛	teaspoon salt
1	teaspoon fresh lemon juice

Combine all the ingredients. This may be molded or served in a pretty bowl. Serve with chips, pita, rye bread, or crackers.

YIELD: 6 TO 8 SERVINGS

New York Strip Steak Roast

For those who remember when we always served roast beef and for those who still do, the flavor of this roast is just wonderful. It is my favorite cut of beef, both in a steak and a roast. You may have to ask your butcher to cut it for you. I always use a good table wine for cooking.

Preheat oven to 350°. Wash and dry the meat. Season it well with Lawry's seasoned salt, ground black pepper, and pat on lots of caraway seed.

Place in a roasting pan and roast uncovered for 18 to 20 minutes per pound for rare, or use a meat thermometer for accurate testing.

When done, remove from pan to a cutting board and allow it to set up for at least 10 minutes. Combine the red wine and chili sauce in a saucepan. Bring to a boil and simmer for 10 minutes. Add it to the drippings in the pan and pour over the meat after slicing.

1	strip steak roast, about ½ pound per person
	Lawry's seasoned salt
	ground black pepper
	caraway seed
1	cup red wine
½	cup chili sauce

Cherry-Glazed Cornish Hens

I like to serve these small hens but they can be very messy; I have found that it is nicer to cut them in half before baking. It is not too difficult if you use a very sharp knife or poultry shears. While I rarely freeze prepared foods, I often make a large batch of these and freeze them with some gravy in dinner portions. When ready to use, defrost and heat in a 325° oven for thirty minutes.

4	Cornish hens, split in half
	several garlic cloves, crushed
	ground ginger
	salt
2	16-ounce cans pitted dark sweet cherries and juice
1	teaspoon dried rosemary
⅛	teaspoon dried crushed red pepper
½	cup red wine
⅓	cup dried cherries

Preheat oven to 350°. Place the halves of hens in a roasting pan and season well on both sides with crushed garlic, ginger, and salt.

In a blender or processor, purée the cherries, juice, rosemary, and dried red pepper. In a saucepan, heat the purée and the wine and simmer until sauce becomes thickened. Adjust taste with salt and pepper. Coat hens with some of the sauce, add the dried cherries to the pan, and bake for 1½ hours, basting frequently. They should be generously glazed. Spoon balance of sauce over hens when serving.

YIELD: 6 TO 8 SERVINGS

Baked Farfel

Farfel is a Jewish version of a small pasta. While many originally prepared it and served it in chicken soup, somewhere along the line it became a delicious casserole, which can be used in the place of rice or potatoes. This is my version.

Preheat oven to 350°. Grease a frying pan with olive oil and sauté the mushrooms, pimiento, and onions until onions are glassy. Remove from the stove and add the butter.

Combine the cooked farfel with the hot vegetable mixture and add all the seasonings. Blend well.

Pour into a well-greased oven-to-table casserole and bake until hot, 20 to 30 minutes, or heat in a microwave oven.

YIELD: 6 TO 8 SERVINGS

1	12-ounce package of toasted farfel, prepared according to directions on package
1	pound white mushrooms, caps and stems, sliced
1	4-ounce jar sliced pimiento
1	large onion, diced
4	tablespoons butter
¼	teaspoon garlic powder
½	teaspoon curry powder
⅛	teaspoon white pepper
¼	teaspoon Lawry's seasoned salt
	olive oil

Carrot and Sweet Potato Tzimmes

This is a very traditional dish served especially on Rosh Hashanah, because it is sweet. As for me, I could eat this at any time of the year.

12	ounces frozen apple juice, undiluted
4	ounces frozen orange juice, undiluted
¼	cup fresh lemon juice
2	teaspoons kosher salt
½	cup brown sugar (or 2 teaspoons Sweet 'n Low)
¼	teaspoon ground cardamom
8	whole black peppercorns
½	cup water
2	pounds sirloin or filet mignon or flat cut brisket
2	pounds fresh or frozen sliced carrots
4	large sweet potatoes, cut into chunks

In a large pot, place the apple juice, orange juice, and lemon juice. Add the salt, sugar, cardamom, and peppercorns. Add the ½ cup water. Bring to a boil and add the meat. Cook until almost tender. Add the carrots and potatoes. Cook until tender, and almost all the liquid has been absorbed–about one hour.

For a stronger flavor, adjust with salt and lemon juice, a little at a time.

Serve hot.

YIELD: 8 TO 10 SERVINGS AS A SIDE DISH

Hot Vegetable Bouquet

I must be honest and tell you that as youngsters my children did not appreciate fresh vegetables. However, I was always delighted when vegetables were served unadorned. Just sprinkle some fresh lemon juice or a little seasoned rice vinegar over them and I am happy.

As your centerpiece in the middle of your platter, use a whole head of steamed cauliflower.

Surround it with steamed carrots, string beans, or zucchini, keeping color in mind.

If you feel the veggies should have a topping of some kind, sprinkle some toasted seasoned bread crumbs mixed with a little olive oil over them, after you have used the lemon juice or vinegar.

YIELD: AT LEAST 10 SERVINGS

Apricot Mold

Molds were regulars on our holiday tables for many years. If you use sugar-free gelatin, always add a little fresh lemon juice to cut the artificial sweet taste.

1	large (6-ounce) package lemon gelatin
2	cups boiling water
½	cup cold water
1	can (12 ounces) Solo apricot filling (usually found in the kosher food section of your supermarket)

Dissolve gelatin in hot water. Add cold water. Allow to cool.

Add apricot filling and place in blender and whip.

Pour into a greased mold. Chill until firm. Unmold, garnish with seasonal fresh fruit, and serve.

YIELD: 6 TO 8 SERVINGS

Plum Kuchen

I prefer kuchens to pies or cakes. This is an old Viennese recipe. Since Italian plums are in season for such a short time, it's a nice idea to make several of these and freeze them raw. What fun eating a plum kuchen in the middle of winter!

Preheat oven to 425°.

Mix flour, sugar, and salt. Cut in butter until mixture resembles coarse crumbs. Add egg yolks and vanilla; mix just until a soft dough is formed.

Grease a 10-inch springform pan. Press dough over bottom and up 1 inch of the sides of the springform pan. Spread nuts over the dough. Arrange the plums over the dough, overlapping wedges.

For topping, mix sugar and flour; cut in butter until mixture resembles coarse crumbs. Stir in vanilla. Sprinkle over plums.

Bake on the lowest oven rack for 15 minutes. Reduce temperature to 400°; bake for 20 to 25 minutes, or until golden brown. Cool in pan on wire rack for about 10 minutes. Remove side of pan; cool completely on wire rack. Serve with sweetened whipped cream.

YIELD: 10 TO 12 SERVINGS

1¾ cups flour
½ cup sugar
dash of salt
¼ pound plus 3 tablespoons unsalted butter
3 egg yolks (extra large)
1 teaspoon vanilla extract
½ cup medium-ground almonds
1½ pounds Italian blue plums, pitted and cut into ¼-inch-thick wedges

TOPPING

⅓ cup sugar
1 cup flour
5 tablespoons unsalted butter, chilled
½ teaspoon vanilla extract

Apple Kuchen

This European type of dessert is still a favorite with every generation. I make several at a time, but do not bake them. I freeze them raw, and when I need one, I take it out of the freezer and bake it.

KUCHEN DOUGH

1½   cups flour

¼   cup sugar

½   teaspoon baking powder

12   tablespoons butter

3   tablespoons orange juice

1   teaspoon vanilla extract

FILLING

8 to 10 Granny Smith apples, peeled and sliced

⅓   cup fresh lemon juice

¼   cup sugar

⅓   cup flour

STREUSEL TOPPING

¾   cup sugar

3   tablespoons flour

2   tablespoons butter

½   teaspoon cinnamon

Place all the ingredients for the dough in a food processor and process until it forms a ball. Remove from processor, wrap in waxed paper, and refrigerate for at least one hour.

For the filling, toss the fruit with the fresh lemon juice. Then toss with the sugar and flour to coat well.

Blend topping ingredients in a food processor until crumbly.

Preheat oven to 350°. Press the dough into a 10-inch pie plate or tart pan. Crimp edges if using a pie plate. Sprinkle the bottom of the crust with some of the streusel topping.

Arrange the fruit in the pastry crust spiral fashion. Cover generously with the streusel topping.

Bake for 45 minutes, or until crust is browned. If baking frozen kuchen, allow additional time.

YIELD: 6 TO 8 SERVINGS

Yom Kippur

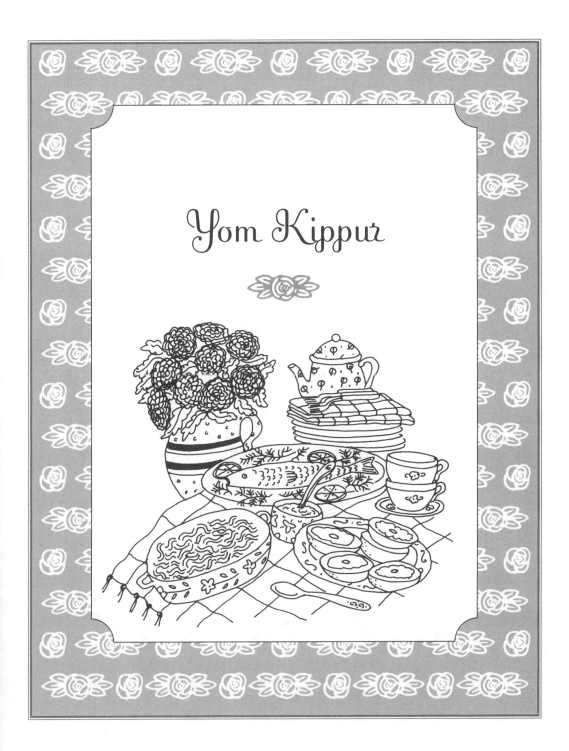

Yom Kippur

Yom Kippur, the Day of Atonement for the Jewish people, is the holiest day of the year. It is difficult for some, as we fast the whole day.

Families begin this holiday in different ways. In anticipation of the fast, some have a large meal the night the holiday begins, while others have a very light meal. In our family, we have always had a rather bland meal such as a broiled steak, plain baked potato, salad (no dressing), and applesauce. The next day is usually spent in prayer at the temple, and at sundown we all rush to the bountiful meal we have come to expect at the end of this holiday.

As you can see from the following suggested menu, our family has customarily served a dairy meal. However, this is our choice and does not have to be yours.

If you are serving bagels, lox, and cream cheese, have the bakery slice the bagels in advance so that you just have to heat and serve. You may want to purchase the lox, or you may want to refer to the lox recipe in my first book, *Grandma Doralee Patinkin's Jewish Family Cookbook.*

Yom Kippur Buffet

Tomato/V-8/Orange Juice

Bagels, Lox, and Cream Cheese
Cold Roasted Salmon with Cucumber Sauce
Herring in Sour Cream

Tunafish Salad
and/or
Fresh Salmon Salad

Gefilte Fish Mold with Red Horseradish

Pineapple Noodle Pudding

Sliced Vegetable Tray

Fresh Marinated Fruit Salad

Coffee and Tea

See my Sweet Table chapter for desserts.

Cold Roasted Salmon

This takes far less time than poaching and is wonderful served cold with cucumber sauce on the side. I have found this method of preparing salmon absolutely foolproof and recommend it for many occasions. The fish can be prepared a day or two in advance and carefully wrapped in plastic wrap. Store in the refrigerator until ready to serve.

Preheat oven to 450°. Place fish on a greased baking dish. Sprinkle lightly with Beau Monde seasoning, a little fresh lemon juice, and the snipped dill. Place in the oven and bake for 18 to 20 minutes, depending upon thickness. Remove from oven and allow to cool. As noted above, wrap in plastic wrap.

When ready to serve, trim away the very flat edge and cut the fish vertically. Then cut into squares for serving. Garnish with some white and red radicchio or spring greens and serve with cucumber sauce.

whole fillets of salmon, as thick as possible, center cuts preferred
Beau Monde seasoning
fresh lemon juice
snipped sprigs of fresh dill
white and red radicchio or spring greens

YIELD: ONE FILLET OF SALMON, CUT INTO SQUARES, SHOULD YIELD 16 TO 18 SERVINGS

Cucumber Sauce

1	large European-type cucumber, halved and seeded, cut into chunks
½	cup mayonnaise, regular or low fat
½	cup sour cream, regular or low fat
½	teaspoon Dijon mustard
1	tablespoon fresh lemon juice
1	tablespoon chives or finely cut green onion
1	heaping tablespoon snipped fresh dill

Place all the ingredients in the food processor. Blend with pulsating motion. Do not overprocess as mixture will become too watery.

This should be made in advance so that the ingredients blend well.

YIELD: ABOUT 1½ CUPS

Herring in Sour Cream

This old favorite is welcome at any time of the year, but is a must for my Yom Kippur buffet. It should be made a day or two in advance. Serve in a beautiful bowl large enough to accommodate the sauce.

Put the herring in a bowl, add the other ingredients, and add ⅓ cup of the reserved liquid. Return to a large container and stir occasionally.

YIELD: 8 TO 12 SERVINGS

1	32-ounce jar Nathan's herring snacks in wine sauce, drained, but reserve liquid
1	large sweet onion, thinly sliced
1	large sweet apple (do not peel), cut into small slices
1	teaspoon sugar
2	cups sour cream

Tunafish Salad

Toasted pine nuts add a lot to this old favorite. I mold this either in a fish mold or in a ring mold and then garnish.

½	cup pine nuts
2	6-ounce cans water-packed white tuna
4	celery ribs, finely diced
1	tablespoon fresh lemon juice
½	cup diced red bell pepper
⅛	teaspoon white pepper
1	teaspoon dried dill
1	tablespoon dried minced onions
½	cup mayonnaise

Toast the pine nuts at about 250° in your toaster oven. Stir occasionally. Watch carefully.

Drain the tuna and put in a large bowl. Combine all the ingredients and blend well. Mold and refrigerate for at least 4 hours

Unmold and garnish.

YIELD: 6 SERVINGS

Fresh Salmon Salad

There is a tremendous difference between salmon salad made with fresh and canned salmon. Whenever I have any of my roasted salmon left over, I always prepare this, which is my husband's favorite.

Just take the leftover salmon, mash it with a fork, add some mayonnaise and sweet pickle relish, and enjoy!

Gefilte Fish Mold with Red Horseradish

This is an excellent appetizer as well as a nice first course. I also use this at my Yom Kippur buffet instead of preparing the traditional gefilte fish. It's colorful and delicious.

1½ 24-ounce jars gefilte fish, drained (save liquid) and cut into thick slices

1 large package lemon Jell-O

2 cups boiling water

1 cup fish liquid

1 small jar red horseradish

juice of ½ lemon

spring greens for garnish

Combine the Jell-O with the boiling water and fish liquid. Stir until completely dissolved. Add horseradish to gelatin and blend.

Pour some gelatin into a ring mold and chill until firm.

Place the slices of fish vertically over the chilled gelatin and pour the balance of the gelatin mixture over the fish. Chill until very firm.

Garnish a platter with some spring greens and unmold.

YIELD: 10 TO 12 SERVINGS

Pineapple Noodle Pudding

I have always loved the pineapple flavor of this kugel. When I do not have to concern myself with the dietetic needs of others, I turn to an old favorite. From the kitchen of my dear friend, Shirley Krieberg.

Preheat oven to 350°. Beat egg whites into peaks and set aside. Combine butter, sugar, salt, and egg yolks and beat until thick and creamy. Add crushed pineapple, noodles, and raisins and mix well.

Fold in the beaten egg whites. Pour into a greased oven-to-table baking dish about 8½ x 11 inches.

Bake for 45 to 50 minutes.

YIELD: 8 TO 12 SERVINGS

4	eggs (room temperature), separated
¼	pound butter
1¼	cups sugar
½	teaspoon salt
1	20-ounce can crushed pineapple, drained well
1	pound semi-broad noodles (cooked according to instructions on package, drained, and rinsed with cold water)
1	cup raisins

Sliced Vegetable Tray

Unadorned vegetables are the best for this occasion. We usually serve:

sliced beefsteak tomatoes

sliced sweet onions

sliced English cucumbers

radish roses

Greek olives

marinated artichoke hearts

Arrange the vegetables decoratively on a large platter and garnish with parsley or kale.

Fresh Marinated Fruit Salad

I always have fruit on my table. I am not giving you specific quantities, as I believe you have to be the judge of how much you will need and it will depend on what is available that particular season. Leftover marinated fruit salad is delicious the next day.

Choose your fruits and place them in a large deep container that has a tight lid. Marinate the watermelon separately and add just before serving, as it creates too much liquid.

Add the orange juice, ginger, cloves, brown sugar, and Grand Marnier. Toss occasionally. This should marinate for several hours in the refrigerator.

When ready to serve, add the watermelon and the toasted pecans.

assorted melons, cut into thick chunks (you do not want it to get mushy)

watermelon, cut up but set aside

grapes

berries (strawberries, raspberries, blueberries)

fresh peaches, sliced

fresh plums, sliced

fresh nectarines, sliced

pears, sliced

small amount of orange juice (enough to coat all the fruit)

ground ginger, to taste

ground cloves, to taste

brown sugar, to taste, or Sweet'n Low

Grand Marnier, to taste

toasted pecan halves

Thanksgiving

Thanksgiving

I think Thanksgiving is one of the most enjoyable holidays of the year, a time for rejoicing.

When my children were young, we would all rise very early. I would set off to the kitchen to start preparations for the day, and they would settle down to watch the Macy's holiday parade. This became a Thanksgiving Day ritual in our home. Little did I dream that someday Mandy would be living in New York and taking his children to watch the parade. Both sides of the family always gathered at our home when they were able to make it, and these are the memories I shall always cherish.

When I married into the Rubin clan, my children had left Chicago, so we always celebrated Thanksgiving at the home of Bonnie and Neal Rubin. Her parents would come in from St. Louis, and the entire Rubin clan and extended families would be present. It was Bonnie's father, Charles Segall, who insisted that a turkey should be roasted "breast down." He was an excellent cook. He is no longer with us, but I always think of him at Thanksgiving, carving the turkey and saving the wings for me.

Well, now we are living out West and, once again, Thanksgiving is always celebrated with close family and our friends of some fifty years, Bella and Marshall Smith and their families. Sometimes we celebrate at home, but sometimes we "make a reservation."

I have always prepared a traditional menu for Thanksgiving and hope the following suggestions may be of help in planning yours.

Thanksgiving

Bruschetta
Spinach-Mushroom Crescents
Cream Cheese Torta

Roasted Boneless Turkey Breast

Wild Rice Stuffing and/or
Cranberry Couscous

Sweet Potato Soufflé
Grandma Ida's Candied Sweet Potatoes
and/or Mashed Potatoes

String Beans and Walnuts
and/or Creamed Spinach

Grandma Doralee's Cranberry Sauce
and also
Sugar-Free Cranberry Sauce

Devil's Food Cake with Chocolate Ganache
Pumpkin-Cheese Log
Lemon Pie

Bruschetta

This is becoming very popular as a hearty appetizer. While it is often featured in Italian restaurants, I think it is a marvelous preamble to any meal.

Combine tomatoes and ¼ cup of the chopped basil in a large plastic colander. Sprinkle generously with salt and allow to drain for about 1 hour.

Place the garlic cloves in a small baking dish and brush with a little olive oil. Roast in your toaster oven until soft when pierced. Cool and coarsely chop. Combine garlic with the remaining olive oil. Add the oregano and thyme and tomato mixture. Blend well. Season well with salt and pepper.

Cut the bread slices into fourths and grill or toast them until golden brown on both sides.

Spoon some tomato mixture over each piece. Top with a sprig of basil or a touch of grated mozzarella cheese.

YIELD: 12 TO 24 SERVINGS

12 to 15 plum tomatoes, seeded and diced
½ cup chopped fresh basil
6 large garlic cloves
½ cup olive oil
¾ teaspoon fresh oregano
¾ teaspoon fresh thyme
salt and pepper to taste
6 large slices country bread about 1 inch thick
fresh basil sprigs
mozzarella cheese

Spinach-Mushroom Crescents

Quick and easy and sooo delicious!

1	envelope onion soup mix
2	eggs
1	10-ounce package frozen chopped spinach, cooked and drained
1	4-ounce can sliced mushrooms, drained
2	cups ricotta cheese
1	cup shredded Monterey Jack cheese
3	packages refrigerated crescent rolls

Preheat oven to 350°

In a food processor, combine all of the ingredients, except the rolls, and blend well. Set aside.

Separate crescent rolls according to package directions and then cut each crescent in half. Spoon approximately 1 heaping teaspoon of the spinach-cheese mixture in the center of each crescent and roll from wide end down to the tip.

Place on a parchment-covered baking sheet. Bake for 15 minutes, or until crusts are a golden brown.

YIELD: 48 PIECES

Cream Cheese Torta

My granddaughter Lainie specifically requested that I include a recipe for a torta in this book. This is delicious and simple and is based on a recipe published in a magazine several years ago. As usual, I made a few changes.

Combine the cream cheese and the salad dressing mix and set aside. Combine the artichokes, parsley, and peppers.

Line a 3-cup bowl with plastic wrap. Alternate layers of cream cheese mixture and vegetable mixture, beginning and ending with the cheese mixture. Chill at least 4 hours or overnight.

When ready to serve, invert onto a serving plate and remove the plastic wrap. Garnish and serve with crackers, chips, or toasted pita triangles.

YIELD: 8 TO 10 SERVINGS

2   *8-ounce packages cream cheese*

1   *package ranch salad dressing mix*

1   *6-ounce jar marinated artichokes, drained and coarsely chopped*

1   *tablespoon chopped fresh parsley*

⅓   *cup marinated roasted red peppers, drained and coarsely chopped*

GARNISH

pulled pieces of butter lettuce or some Belgian endive

Roasted Boneless Turkey Breast

I usually purchase a large fresh turkey breast, with the bone in, and have the butcher bone it. Ask for the bones. They can be stored in the freezer and used for a delicious soup whenever you have time after the holiday.

1	whole boneless turkey breast, with skin on
	ground ginger, fresh minced garlic, or granulated garlic powder
⅔	cup apricot preserves
3	tablespoons Dijon mustard
½	cup light soy sauce

The night before:

Season both sides of the turkey breast well with ground ginger and garlic. Put in a roasting pan.

Combine the apricot preserves, mustard, and soy sauce. Blend well and cover the breast, top and bottom, with the sauce. Cover with plastic wrap and refrigerate overnight.

Thanksgiving morning:

Preheat oven to 325°.

Add ¼ cup water to the pan and bake uncovered for 2½ hours, basting occasionally with gravy in pan. Allow to stand for at least 10 minutes before slicing.

YIELD: AT LEAST 12 DINNER SERVINGS

Wild Rice Stuffing

Nothing could be simpler. Use this as a side dish or a stuffing. It is delicious.

To the cooked rice, add the water chestnuts, cherries or cranberries, and the additional butter.

Transfer to an oven-to-table casserole. This can be prepared in advance and reheated in the microwave.

YIELD: 8 SERVINGS

1   *package Uncle Ben's wild rice mix (prepare according to instructions on package)*

1   *5- to 6-ounce can sliced water chestnuts*

½   *cup dried sour cherries or cranberries*

2   *additional tablespoons butter*

Cranberry Couscous

This is a delicious version of this most versatile grainlike pasta. It can be used as a side dish with your turkey in place of the usual bread stuffing.

2	cups frozen apple juice concentrate
1	cup water
½	teaspoon ground cloves
½	teaspoon ground cinnamon
½	teaspoon salt
1½	cups dried cranberries
2	cups quick-cooking couscous
3	tablespoons butter
½	cup minced green onions

In a saucepan, combine the liquid, seasonings, and cranberries. Bring to a boil. Remove from heat and add the couscous, butter, and green onion. Cover and allow to stand for 6 minutes. Before serving, fluff with a fork.

This can be made in advance, transferred to a serving dish, and heated in the microwave.

YIELD: 8 TO 10 SERVINGS

Sweet Potato Soufflé

For those who want a change from the traditional candied sweets, this is a holiday delight. I prefer using garnet sweet potatoes.

Preheat oven to 375°.

Beat the egg whites until stiff and set aside. Place the sweet potatoes in a food processor and blend slightly. Add the brown sugar, orange juice, butter, salt, spices, and egg yolks and process until well blended. Pour the sweet potato mixture over the beaten whites and fold in carefully. Pour into an oven-to-table casserole about 9 x 13 inches, or an average round Pyrex casserole.

For the topping, combine all the ingredients and sprinkle over the sweet potato mixture.

Bake for 45 to 60 minutes, until firm and puffy.

YIELD: 10 TO 12 SERVINGS

4	eggs, separated
8	medium sweet potatoes, peeled and boiled until tender
1	cup solidly packed brown sugar
¼	cup orange juice
2	tablespoons butter
1	teaspoon salt
½	teaspoon ground ginger
¼	teaspoon ground cloves

TOPPING

¼	cup brown sugar
½	cup crushed cornflakes
½	cup chopped pecans
2	tablespoons butter, melted

Grandma Ida's Candied Sweet Potatoes

While this recipe appeared in my first book, it is one that was handed down from my mother, and Thanksgiving would not be the same without Grandma Ida's candied sweet potatoes.

8	medium sweet potatoes

GLAZE

1	cup solidly packed brown sugar
⅓	cup fresh orange juice
1	tablespoon butter
1	teaspoon salt

In a covered pan, steam the potatoes in a small amount of water, only until you can easily remove the skin.

Cut the potatoes into halves or quarters and place them in a well-greased baking dish. Preheat oven to 350°.

To make the glaze, combine the brown sugar, orange juice, butter, and salt in a medium-size saucepan and cook for at least 5 minutes, or until clear.

Pour this glaze over the potatoes and bake for 45 minutes, basting several times. When done, they should be well glazed, or candied.

YIELD: 8 TO 12 SERVINGS

Note ❀ For a sugar-free recipe, omit the glaze and use a sugar-free maple syrup (available in any supermarket). Sprinkle potatoes with a little orange juice and a touch of ground cloves and ground ginger and pour the syrup over the potatoes. Bake as you would the others.

Mashed Potatoes

Who doesn't like good old-fashioned mashed potatoes? Yukon Golds are especially moist and sweet. If unavailable, reds are an excellent substitute. I prefer a processor or electric mixer, but an old-fashioned masher will do just as well.

In a large pot, cover potatoes and onion with some salted water and bring to a boil. Cover and cook until tender.

Drain the potatoes and onion and transfer to your mixer or processor. Heat the milk or broth and the butter and add to the potatoes. Blend until smooth. Season with salt and pepper.

YIELD: 4 TO 6 SERVINGS

3   pounds Yukon Gold potatoes or red potatoes, peeled and cut into large pieces

1   medium onion, cut into chunks

1   cup hot milk (for lower fat content, use 1 cup chicken broth)

1   tablespoon butter, margarine, or olive oil

    salt and pepper to taste

String Beans and Walnuts

This has to be made just before serving, but it takes only a few minutes. Wonderful as an accompaniment to beef as well as Thanksgiving turkey or other poultry.

1	tablespoon peanut oil
1	cup coarsely chopped walnuts (pecans can be substituted)
1	pound whole French string beans
1 to 2	tablespoons soy sauce
½	teaspoon garlic powder
⅛	teaspoon white pepper

Heat the peanut oil and lightly brown the walnut pieces. Add the string beans and sauté for a few minutes. Add the soy sauce, garlic powder, and pepper. Toss well and serve.

YIELD: 4 TO 6 SERVINGS

Creamed Spinach

It is so seldom that children love spinach, but my grandson Isaac has always loved creamed spinach. This is my version.

In a large pan of boiling salted water, cook spinach for 2 minutes and drain, pressing out as much water as possible.

In a skillet, cook onion in butter until softened. Blend in spinach, cream, pepper, nutmeg, and salt. Cook until most of the cream is absorbed.

YEILD: 4 TO 6 SERVINGS

2   *pounds fresh spinach, stems discarded, coarsely chopped*

2   *large sweet onions, minced*

2   *tablespoons sweet butter*

½   *cup heavy cream*

¼   *teaspoon ground black pepper*

¼   *teaspoon ground nutmeg*

  salt to taste

Grandma Doralee's Cranberry Sauce

There are many recipes for cranberry sauce, but this is one of my favorites. When cranberries are in season, make a large quantity and freeze it in small quantities, so that you have it all year.

3   12-ounce bags fresh
    cranberries

2   cups frozen apple
    juice, undiluted

1   cup water

1½ cups brown sugar

1   teaspoon freshly
    grated ginger

1   teaspoon ground
    cloves

1½ cups toasted nuts
    (slivered almonds,
    pecans, or walnuts)

Combine all the ingredients, except the nuts, in a large pot. Cover and bring to a boil. Reduce heat to a simmer and cook for 20 to 30 minutes, stirring occasionally. Mixture will thicken. Remove from heat and add the nuts.

Spoon into containers and refrigerate or freeze. Mixture will continue to thicken upon cooling.

YIELD: 18 TO 20 SERVINGS

Sugar-Free Cranberry Sauce

There is no reason why those who have to watch their sugar intake should do without cranberry sauce. Trust me, you will never miss the sugar.

Place all the ingredients, except the nuts, in a deep saucepan and bring to a boil. Reduce heat and boil gently for 10 to 15 minutes, stirring constantly. Remove from heat. Add the toasted walnuts. Sauce will thicken as it cools. The stick of cinnamon can remain in the sauce for a stronger flavor.

This may be frozen.

YIELD: 12 SERVINGS

1½	pounds fresh cranberries, washed
1	12-ounce can frozen apple juice, undiluted
½	can cold water
¼	teaspoon ground cloves
¼	teaspoon freshly grated ginger
1	cinnamon stick
2	teaspoons Twin brown sugar substitute
5	teaspoons Sweet'n Low
1	cup toasted walnuts

Devil's Food Chocolate Cake

This is rich and chocolaty, a great favorite. When my children were young I must have baked this cake at least once a week.

6	tablespoons Droste's cocoa
1⅛	teaspoons baking soda
6	tablespoons cool water
2	cups sifted cake flour
¼	teaspoon salt
¼	pound butter
1½	scant cups sugar
2	large eggs
1	teaspoon vanilla extract
¾	cup buttermilk

Preheat oven to 325°.

Mix cocoa, baking soda, and water together. Set aside.

Mix flour and salt together. Set aside.

Blend butter and sugar. Add eggs, one at a time, beating until light and creamy. Add vanilla.

Add flour alternately with the buttermilk, beginning and ending with the flour. Do not overbeat.

Add cocoa mixture and blend well.

Pour into a lightly greased and floured 8-inch or 9-inch square pan, or a slightly larger oblong pan. Bake for 45 minutes; raise heat to 375° and bake for an additional 15 minutes. Always test with a toothpick. Do not overbake. If using a larger pan, reduce your baking time. Remember, always test.

Remove from oven and allow to cool on a cake rack for about 10 minutes; then invert onto cake plate.

When cool, cover with a chocolate frosting or my Chocolate Ganache.

YIELD: 8 TO 10 SERVINGS

Chocolate Ganache

This can be used over a chocolate cake, plain cheesecake, brownies, or any other sweet you want to enhance.

Combine bittersweet and milk chocolate in a large bowl. Set aside. In a 2-quart saucepan, heat cream to boiling point. Pour over chocolate in bowl; allow to stand for about 1 minute. Take a wooden spoon or rubber spatula and gently mix the chocolate and cream until smooth. If chocolate does not melt completely, place bowl over some simmering hot water and mix just until chocolate melts. Add the butter or margarine and mix until very smooth.

8	*ounces bittersweet chocolate, very finely chopped*
3	*ounces milk chocolate, very finely chopped*
1	*cup heavy or whipping cream*
4	*tablespoons butter or margarine, cut up*

If using the ganache immediately, place bowl in an ice bath (a container filled with water and ice cubes) and stir occasionally with spatula until mixture thickens and is of spreading consistency. This may take about 20 minutes.

If you are not using the ganache immediately, instead of the ice bath, place it in the refrigerator for at least 4 hours or overnight. When ready to use, allow ganache to come to room temperature for spreading consistency.

YIELD: ENOUGH FOR A 10-INCH CAKE

Pumpkin-Cheese Log

This is a delicious Thanksgiving dessert. My daughter Joanne always prepares this for our dessert table and it has become a favorite with our family.

3	large eggs
1	cup sugar
⅔	cup mashed pumpkin (canned)
1	teaspoon fresh lemon juice
¾	cup flour
1	teaspoon baking powder
2	teaspoons cinnamon
½	teaspoon nutmeg
¼	teaspoon allspice
¼	teaspoon salt
1	cup chopped pecans
	powdered sugar

Preheat oven to 375°.

Grease a 15½ x 10½ x 1-inch jelly roll pan. Line with baking parchment or waxed paper and spray the paper with a cooking spray.

In mixing bowl of an electric mixer, beat eggs and sugar until thick and creamy, approximately 4 minutes. Mix in pumpkin and lemon juice.

In a separate bowl, mix all the dry ingredients, except the nuts and powdered sugar, together. Fold into pumpkin mixture. Pour into prepared pan. Smooth batter. Sprinkle chopped nuts over batter. Bake for approximately 14 minutes. Cake should spring back when lightly pressed with finger.

Once the cake is in the oven, place a clean dish towel on a flat surface. Sprinkle with powdered sugar until covered, but not too thick. Remove cake from oven and immediately place cake upside down on towel. Roll the cake in the towel, starting from the narrow end, and set aside, seam side down. Allow to cool completely.

While cake is cooling, mix together cream cheese and butter until light and fluffy. Mix in powdered sugar and vanilla. When cake is cool, unroll and remove towel. Spread cheese filling over the top of the cake, making sure that you spread all the way to the ends. Roll up the cake again and place seam side down. Refrigerate for several hours or overnight.

Can be wrapped in foil and frozen.

YIELD: 10 SERVINGS

CHEESE FILLING

8	ounces cream cheese, at room temperature
4	tablespoons butter, at room temperature
1¼	cups powdered sugar
1	teaspoon vanilla extract

Lemon Pie

There is nothing more delicious than a tart lemon pie topped with toasted chopped almonds and whipped cream.

PIE CRUST

12	tablespoons butter
1	cup flour
⅓	cup powdered sugar
⅛	teaspoon salt
1	pound dried baby lima beans

FILLING

3	large eggs
¾	cup sugar
⅓	cup fresh lemon juice
3	teaspoons grated fresh lemon rind
6	tablespoons butter at room temperature
1	cup toasted chopped almonds

Preheat oven to 350°. Melt butter in a 9- or 10-inch pie plate. When hot, stir in flour, powdered sugar, and salt. Blend well. Press into place, bringing the dough up the sides. Fill the center with dried baby lima beans to prevent shrinking and bake until golden brown. Cool on a rack.

Place all filling ingredients, except the butter and toasted almonds, in a saucepan or double boiler. Blend well with a whisk. Place over low heat and cook, stirring constantly with a wooden spoon, until mixture thickens. As it comes to a boil, remove from heat. Add butter and cool. Spoon into baked pie shell.

Refrigerate for several hours so that filling becomes firm and flavors blend. May be refrigerated overnight.

Garnish with toasted chopped almonds and serve with whipped cream.

YIELD: 8 SERVINGS

Hanukkah

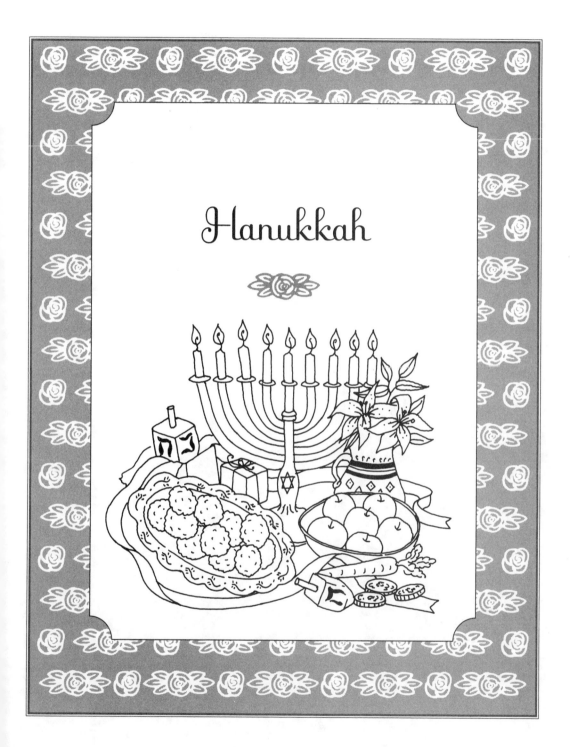

Hanukkah

My daughter's birthday often fell during Hanukkah. Our house was always decorated for Hanukkah and so her little non-Jewish friends were introduced to the Miracle of Miracles—the festival of the lights. What a wonderful time of year—eight days of celebrating, exchanging gifts with family and friends. How well I remember the excitement of lighting the menorah every night and singing the prayers. I did it as a child, my children did it, and the tradition carries on with my grandchildren.

Let us always "keep the faith" and watch their eyes shine as brightly as the Hanukkah candles.

Hanukkah

Chutney Monterey
Artichoke Niblets
Mushroom Rolls

Pot-Roasted Hamburger
and/or
Oven-Fried Chicken

Potato Latkes with Doralee's
Chunky Cranberry-Apple Sauce
and/or
Zucchini and Carrot Latkes

Sweet-and-Sour Cucumbers
and/or
Pickled Beet Salad Mold

Party Cheesecake with Raspberry Sauce

Chocolate Pecan Angel Food Cake

Chutney Monterey

The combination of chutney and Jack cheese is unusual and delicious. This is from the kitchen of my daughter, Marsha Patinkin Schwartzman.

In a food processor, blend the chutney and the cheese well. Spread on the toasted rounds. Sprinkle with the crushed Baco Bits and broil until hot.

YIELD: APPROXIMATELY 12 SERVINGS

9   ounces Major Grey's chutney

½   pound Monterey Jack cheese

Rounds or small squares of crustless white bread, lightly toasted

½   cup Baco Bits, crushed

Artichoke Niblets

This is an old recipe that is delicious hot or cold. It can be made ahead and frozen raw. Bake when ready to serve.

1	small onion, cut up
1	garlic clove, chopped
2	6-ounce jars marinated artichokes (drain oil and save)
3	eggs
¼	cup seasoned bread crumbs
2	cups shredded Cheddar cheese
2	tablespoons chopped fresh parsley
½	teaspoon salt
⅛	teaspoon pepper
1	teaspoon oregano
	Tabasco sauce to taste
	Parmesan cheese for topping

Preheat oven to 350°.

Sauté onion and garlic in a little of the oil drained from the artichokes.

Place all the ingredients, except the Parmesan, in a food processor and blend well with pulsating action. Adjust seasonings to taste.

Grease a 7 x 11-inch pan. Spread ingredients evenly in pan. Sprinkle with Parmesan cheese and bake for 30 minutes.

To serve, cut into small squares.

YIELD: 24 SERVINGS

Mushroom Rolls

Oh, how my family loved these! My Aunt Ethel gave me this recipe. It was a winner years ago and I think it still is. Low cholesterol it isn't.

Remove crusts from bread and roll each slice as flat as possible.

Melt the butter in a frying pan and sauté the mushrooms and onion for a few minutes. Add the cream cheese and blend very well.

Add the egg yolks, garlic powder, salt, and pepper and cook over low heat until mixture is thick.

Place in refrigerator to cool.

Spread each slice of bread with mixture and roll up tightly. At this point, you can either freeze these rolls or fry them at once, and then freeze them.

Fry them in hot peanut oil until golden brown. Drain them very well on paper towels. Cut each roll into thirds (or halves).

When ready to serve, heat in a toaster oven at 325°.

YIELD: 48 PIECES

1	24-ounce sandwich loaf of plain white bread
4	tablespoons butter
¾	pound mushrooms, chopped
1	small onion, chopped
8	ounces cream cheese
2	egg yolks
¼	teaspoon garlic powder
¼	teaspoon salt
⅛	teaspoon pepper
	peanut oil for frying

Pot-Roasted Hamburger

As a young bride, I made this for Grandpa Max and Grandma Celia. Thereafter, whenever I came to their house I prepared this for dinner.

Although we've cut down on our meat dinners, this is still one of my favorites and it freezes quite well. Just thaw and heat in the microwave. Serve with a green salad and applesauce and you have a complete meal.

MEAT

- 3 pounds (extra lean) ground beef
- 1 package herb-seasoned soup mix
- 3 eggs (or ¼ cup egg substitute)
- ½ cup bread crumbs, cornflake crumbs, or matzo meal
- ½ cup chili sauce
- ½ cup water
- 1 teaspoon garlic powder

Mix the first seven ingredients together and form into balls the size of golf balls. Set aside.

Place the tomatoes, water, broth, bay leaf, salt, curry powder, garlic, basil, sun-dried tomatoes, pepper, mushrooms, and onion in a deep Dutch oven. Bring sauce to a boil, reduce heat, and cook for about 10 minutes. Add the meatballs, carrots, and the potatoes. Bring to a boil again and reduce to a low heat. Cook for about 1½ hours, basting while cooking. Allow gravy to thicken.

YIELD: 6 TO 8 SERVINGS

SAUCE

1	28 to 30-ounce can peeled plum or pear tomatoes
1	can water (wash out can)
1	14½-ounce can beef broth
1	bay leaf
1	teaspoon salt
1	teaspoon curry powder
1	teaspoon garlic powder, or 4 garlic cloves, chopped
1	teaspoon dried basil
6 to 8	pieces sun-dried tomatoes, cut up
½	teaspoon pepper
6	ounces fresh mushrooms, sliced
1	large onion, cut into chunks
1	pound fresh baby carrots
3 to 4	white potatoes, cut into chunks

Oven-Fried Chicken

This recipe, for many of us, replaced deep-frying. To really minimize the fat, be sure the chicken is skinned. Should you still prefer deep-frying, go for it. Colonel Sanders did.

8	chicken breasts, legs, and/or thighs—bone in
3	egg whites, beaten just until frothy
1	cup crushed corn-flake crumbs
1	tablespoon Lawry's seasoned salt
⅓	cup olive oil for fry-ing—just brush well for oven frying

Preheat oven to 350°.

Season the cornflake crumbs to taste with the Lawry's seasoned salt. Dip the chicken parts in the frothy egg whites and then shake them in the cornflake crumbs. Repeat. Place them on a well-greased pan and brush with olive oil.

Bake for 30 minutes and turn the pieces. Brush again with olive oil. Bake for an additional 30 minutes.

YIELD: ALLOW 1 TO 2 PIECES PER PERSON

Potato Latkes

While this recipe appeared in *Grandma Doralee Patinkin's Jewish Family Cookbook,* what would Hanukkah be without latkes? The food processor has eliminated the hand-grating of the potatoes and has made this traditional holiday favorite quite simple. *Happy Hanukkah!*

Peel potatoes and onion. (If not using immediately, place in cold water.) Cut up and shred with the shredding blade of the food processor.

Put the shredded potatoes in a large strainer and press out liquid. Then pour some cold water over the potatoes and press out liquid once more. Transfer to large mixing bowl.

Beat eggs and egg whites until thick. Add to potato mixture. Add flour, baking powder, and seasonings. Blend well.

Heat oil in frying pan. When ready, drop batter by large metal cooking spoon to give you an oval shape. Fry over moderate to high heat until brown, turning to brown other side. Remove from frying pan and drain on paper towels.

Serve with my chunky cranberry-apple sauce or sour cream.

YIELD: AT LEAST 24 PANCAKES

6	large white potatoes
1	large onion
2	eggs (or ½ cup egg substitute)
2	egg whites
⅓	cup flour or matzo meal
1	teaspoon baking powder
½	teaspoon garlic powder
1	teaspoon salt
½	teaspoon white pepper
	peanut oil for frying

Doralee's Chunky Cranberry-Apple Sauce

Cranberries combined with sweet apples create a sauce sure to please the palate. If you like it sweeter, add more honey. I like a tart sauce.

1	12-ounce bag fresh cranberries
12	McIntosh apples, cored (peeled optional) and cut into chunks
2	cinnamon sticks
	juice of ½ fresh lemon
¼	teaspoon ground cloves
¼	teaspoon ground ginger
½	teaspoon ground cinnamon
½	cup water
½	cup honey
¼	teaspoon salt

Place all ingredients in a 6- to 8-quart saucepan. Cover tightly and bring to a boil. Reduce to medium-low heat and cook for 30 minutes. Stir well. Reduce to low heat and cook another 30 minutes.

Remove from heat and allow to cool.

When serving, remove the cinnamon sticks.

YIELD: 12 TO 16 SERVINGS

Zucchini and Carrot Latkes

Healthy, delicious, and a wonderful complement to almost any meal. My mah-jongg ladies love them. These are a great accompaniment for a light luncheon meal, and are especially festive at Hanukkah time.

Using the shredding blade in a processor, shred the carrots and zucchini. Transfer to a large bowl and add the green onions and beaten eggs. Blend well. Add the balance of the ingredients, except the oil. Adjust seasonings, if necessary.

Spray a large frying pan with a vegetable spray. Add a little peanut oil and with a large oval mixing spoon, drop by spoonfuls into the hot oil. Allow the pancakes to set before turning. When crisp, remove and place on paper toweling to remove any excess oil.

These can be made in advance. Place on a cookie sheet and heat in a 400° oven when ready to serve.

YIELD: 6 SERVINGS

4	*large zucchini*
4	*large carrots*
½	*cup chopped green onions*
4	*eggs, beaten*
½	*cup flour*
1	*heaping teaspoon baking powder*
½	*teaspoon nutmeg*
⅛	*teaspoon cardamom*
½	*teaspoon salt*
⅛	*teaspoon ground pepper*
	peanut oil for frying

Sweet-and-Sour Cucumbers

My husband loves cucumbers prepared almost any way, but this is one of his favorites. These will keep well in a tightly covered glass jar or bowl and are a great complement to almost any meal. If at all possible, purchase the long cucumbers that come from British Columbia, as opposed to those grown in California or Mexico. There is a great difference in texture and flavor.

2	very large English cucumbers, cut into 1-inch slices
1½	cups Marukan seasoned rice vinegar
1½	cups cold water
3	packets artificial sweetener
1	tablespoon dried dill
1	tablespoon dried chives

Combine all ingredients and allow to marinate at least 24 hours before serving.

You can add additional cucumber slices as the first batch is eaten, but I do not like my cukes to become too soft, so I suggest you do it sparingly.

YIELD: 6 TO 8 SERVINGS

Pickled Beet Salad Mold

Beets are not popular with some of my children, but I enjoy them in any form. This particular salad is a most refreshing complement to any entrée.

Dissolve the Jell-O in the boiling water. Add the cold liquid and the balance of the ingredients, except celery and beets. Chill until slightly thick.

Add the diced celery and diced beets and blend well.

Turn into a greased mold and refrigerate overnight.

YIELD: 8 TO 10 SERVINGS

1	6-ounce package lemon Jell-O
2	cups boiling water
1½	cups cold liquid (beet juice and/or water)
1½	teaspoons salt
⅛	teaspoon pepper
4	teaspoons red or white horseradish
4	teaspoons chopped sweet onion
1½	cups diced celery
2	cans pickled beets, diced

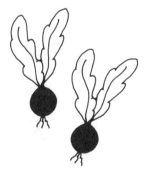

Party Cheesecake

I've never met a cheesecake I didn't like. This classic New York-style cheesecake is delicious served plain, topped with my Raspberry Sauce, or topped with store-bought cherry pie filling.

CRUST

1½ cups graham cracker crumbs

¼ cup sugar

4 tablespoons butter, melted

FILLING

1 cup sugar (divide in half)

3 8-ounce packages cream cheese

juice and grated rind of 2 lemons

4 egg whites (extra large eggs at room temperature)

For the crust, combine the crumbs and sugar with the butter. Press the crumbs into a greased 9-inch springform pan, leaving some crumbs for the top.

For the filling, combine ½ cup of the sugar with the cream cheese and lemon juice and rind. Beat the other ½ cup of sugar with the egg whites until stiff, but not dry. Fold into the cheese mixture.

Pour into the springform pan and sprinkle with the remaining crumbs.

Preheat oven to 325° and bake in center of oven for 45 to 50 minutes. Turn oven off and allow cheesecake to cool in oven for several hours.

YIELD: 10 TO 12 SERVINGS

Raspberry Sauce

In a small saucepan over low heat, combine jam, lemon juice, and liqueur. Stir until hot. Remove from heat and cool. Stir in raspberries.

6	tablespoons seedless raspberry jam
2	tablespoons fresh lemon juice
1	tablespoon strawberry liqueur (optional)
1	cup fresh or frozen raspberries

Chocolate Pecan Angel Food Cake

This is a marvelous angel food cake—one of Auntie Ida's favorites. This cake can also be made for Passover by replacing flour with ¾ cup Passover potato starch and ¼ cup Passover cake meal, and omitting the cream of tartar.

1½	cups egg whites (11 to 13 egg whites)
2	teaspoons cream of tartar
2	tablespoons water
1	teaspoon vanilla extract
1	teaspoon almond or orange extract
1	cup sugar
1	cup sifted flour
¼	teaspoon salt
½	cup Droste's cocoa
1	cup sugar
1	cup chopped pecans

Preheat oven to 375°.

Beat egg whites until frothy and sprinkle cream of tartar over top. Continue beating until stiff enough to hold peaks, but not too dry. Gradually add water and flavorings. Beat in 1 cup sugar, sifting in 1 tablespoon at a time.

Sift the flour, salt, and cocoa together. With a wire whisk, carefully fold the flour mixture into the egg whites, adding the remaining 1 cup of sugar, about ¼ cup at a time. Fold in pecans.

Turn into an ungreased 10-inch, angel food cake pan. Bake for 45 minutes, or until cake tests done. Watch closely for the last 5 minutes, because the top will scorch easily. Invert pan until cake is cool (about 1 hour). Remove from pan and frost.

YIELD: AT LEAST 10 SERVINGS

Holiday Buffet

Holiday Buffet

New Year's Day and Christmas Day were a time when we loved to have all our friends and relatives drop by for cocktails and a buffet supper. As our guests arrived, the table was already set with the appetizers. People would wander about chatting and "grazing" at the table. All concerns about dieting were abandoned. After all, it was holiday time.

After about an hour, we would start removing the "fun food" and start replacing it with a buffet supper. Well into the second hour, as relatives and friends finished eating and began simply visiting, we would start replacing the food with our dessert table. When everyone was ready, they would indulge themselves and relax over a cup of coffee.

From the menu I have selected, you will see that true to my style, I have tried to keep it easy and simple. If you do not care to pull out the china and crystal, you can purchase beautiful party goods and just toss most of it afterward. Try combining fine paper or plastic party goods with some of your own beautiful things. Believe me, it works. I always had as good a time as my guests at these parties, and I hope you will do the same.

Holiday Buffet

The following menu is only a suggestion. You may draw upon the various menus in this book or my <u>Jewish Family Cookbook</u> for anything else you might want to serve. Simply move one phase of the buffet gradually into the next one, ending, of course, with dessert, allowing your guests to linger.

Appetizers

Fresh Veggie Assortment with Tzatziki
Hummus
Eastern Eggplant Dip
Shrimp with Parsley-Dill Sauce
Hot Crabmeat Dip
Mexicali Layered Dip
Roll-Up Appetizers
Stuffed Mushroom Caps

Cocktail Supper

Beef Tenderloin
Plum Chicken or Stuffed Chicken Breasts
Caraway Noodles
Strawberry-Applesauce Mold

Dessert

Please make your selections from my Sweet Table chapter

Fresh Veggie Assortment

These are always a nice complement to a brunch or a buffet table. Some of the veggies I use are as follows:

Arrange veggies according to color, if possible, using sprigs of parsley to separate the clusters. If serving at a cocktail buffet, serve with Tzatziki sauce (see next recipe).

Sliced tomatoes or small cocktail tomatoes

English cucumbers

red and green bell peppers, cut into strips

jicama, cut into slices

radish roses and black olives

whole white mushrooms

cauliflower florets

broccoli florets

baby carrots

celery and zucchini slices

Tzatziki (Cucumber Yogurt Dip)

This is usually served in Greek restaurants with gyros. I think it's great as a dip.

1	English cucumber, peeled, halved lengthwise, and seeded
1	cup whole milk yogurt
1	garlic clove, finely mashed
1	tablespoon extra-virgin olive oil
¼	teaspoon fresh lemon juice
	salt to taste
	cucumber spears (unpeeled) for dipping

Coarsely grate the cucumber. Place on a clean towel and squeeze to remove the juices. Transfer to a bowl. Stir in the yogurt and garlic and then add the olive oil, lemon juice, and salt.

Refrigerate for at least 1 hour (4 hours is ideal).

YIELD: 1½ CUPS

Hummus

This is one of my favorite hummus recipes. You can play around with it and add almost anything you want. Try chopped jicama or anchovies.

Place all the ingredients in a food processor and process until well blended.

Place in refrigerator for several hours. It will thicken as it chills.

Serve with warm or toasted triangles of pita bread.

YIELD: 6 TO 8 SERVINGS

1	15½-ounce can garbanzo beans, drained
¾	cup tahini
¼	cup chopped sun-dried tomatoes (packed in oil)
	oil from sun-dried tomatoes (just enough to obtain the right consistency)
	juice of 1 lemon
1	large garlic clove, peeled and crushed
1	tablespoon chopped parsley
1	teaspoon mild paprika

Eastern Eggplant Dip

An ancient delight. Almost every ethnic menu features some type of eggplant dish, and I am always drawn to it when I see it on a menu. With this one, eggplant lovers will be delighted.

1	large eggplant
3	tablespoons olive oil
1	8-ounce can tomato sauce
2	garlic cloves, minced
1	green pepper, chopped
1	teaspoon ground cumin
⅛	teaspoon cayenne
2	teaspoons sugar
2	teaspoons salt
¼	cup red wine vinegar

Dice eggplant. In a large frying pan, heat oil over medium-high heat. Add eggplant and remaining ingredients. Cover and cook over medium heat for 20 minutes. Uncover and boil mixture over high heat, stirring constantly, until reduced to about 3 cups. Remove from heat. Cover tightly and chill for several hours.

Serve with either plain or toasted pita bread.

YIELD: 10 TO 12 SERVINGS

Shrimp with Parsley-Dill Sauce

This is a real winner! I serve this as an appetizer or as part of a supper buffet. The sauce can also be used as a dip for a fresh veggie platter.

In a food processor, combine parsley, garlic, and dill until well blended. Add onion soup mix, sour cream, mayonnaise, pepper, lemon juice, and curry. Process until smooth.

Chill for several hours and combine with cooked shrimp just before serving.

Forks or toothpicks should be available for the shrimp.

YIELD: 15 TO 20 SERVINGS (3 CUPS SAUCE)

2	bunches of fresh parsley (stems removed), about 4 cups loosely packed
2	medium garlic cloves
1	tablespoon snipped fresh dill
2	envelopes onion soup mix
2	cups sour cream
½	cup mayonnaise
¼	teaspoon pepper
	juice of ½ lemon
½	teaspoon curry powder
4	pounds large shrimp, cooked and deveined

Hot Crabmeat Dip

This recipe has really stood the test of time.

2	8-ounce packages cream cheese
2	tablespoons mayonnaise
3	tablespoons minced dried onions
½	teaspoon salt
¼	teaspoon cayenne
2	tablespoons chopped fresh parsley
1	pound fresh or frozen crabmeat

GARNISH

1	cup sliced toasted almonds

Preheat oven to 375°.

Place all the ingredients, except crabmeat, in a food processor and blend well. Transfer to a bowl. Add the crabmeat and mix well. Pour into an ovenproof serving dish. Top with toasted almonds. Bake for 15 to 20 minutes.

Serve with pita triangles or crackers.

YIELD: 8 TO 10 SERVINGS

Mexicali Layered Dip

One of my favorite appetizers from south of the border. Kids as well as adults go for this in a big way. You can change the choice of vegetables or cheese as you wish. Serve with warm tortilla chips.

Spread the refried beans on a 10-inch serving platter. Combine the sour cream and salad dressing mix and spread over refried beans, making the circle a little smaller so that the beans show. Layer the tomatoes, then the chilies, and then the cheese, always making sure the previous layer shows. Top with the sliced olives.

YIELD: 10 TO 12 SERVINGS

1	16-ounce can refried beans
1	cup sour cream
1	package ranch salad dressing mix
1	cup diced tomatoes
1	4-ounce can green chilies, drained and diced
1½	cups shredded Cheddar cheese
1	2¼-ounce can black olives, drained and sliced

Roll-Up Appetizers

Something new on the scene. I've really taken to the Southwestern cuisine. These can be served plain or dipped in your favorite salsa.

4	ounces cream cheese
1	4-ounce can diced green chilies
½	cup sliced green onions or chives
½	cup chopped black olives
1	cup water-packed white albacore tuna, or cooked turkey or chicken
4	6-inch flour tortillas or soft lavosch crackers

Blend all the ingredients, except tortillas, in a food processor. Spread ½ cup of the mixture on each tortilla. Roll up each tortilla jelly-roll fashion. Wrap each roll in plastic wrap and chill for several hours.

To serve: Cut each roll into 12 slices (½ inch thick).

YIELD: 48 PIECES

Stuffed Mushroom Caps

Stuffed mushrooms make a wonderful appetizer as well as a lovely complement to a meal.

Reserve the mushroom caps. Finely chop the stems.

Heat the oil in a deep skillet. Sauté the onion and finely chopped mushroom stems for a few minutes.

In a large bowl combine the mushroom mixture, cornflake crumbs, garlic, parsley, eggs, and cheese. Blend well.

Stuff the mushroom caps, sprinkle with some additional Cheddar cheese, and bake at 350° until cheese starts to bubble.

These can be served hot or at room temperature.

YIELD: 4 TO 6 SERVINGS

12	*large white mushrooms*
2	*tablespoons olive oil*
2	*cups cornflake crumbs*
1	*sweet onion, diced*
2	*cloves fresh garlic, roasted and minced*
2	*tablespoons minced fresh parsley*
2	*large eggs, slightly beaten*
2	*tablespoons grated Cheddar cheese*
	additional Cheddar cheese for topping

Beef Tenderloin

I love serving this. It's very versatile—I have used it as an entrée, as part of a buffet supper, or in small beef sandwiches that are great on a buffet table. Slice it thick or thin. Serve it hot, serve it cold. It is always wonderful.

1	*whole beef tenderloin, trimmed*
	garlic powder
	Lawry's seasoned salt
	caraway seed
	chili sauce
½	*cup fine red wine*

Preheat oven to 450°.

Season the meat generously on both sides with the garlic powder, Lawry's seasoned salt, and caraway seed. Frost with your favorite chili sauce and add the wine to the pan.

Bake for 25 minutes for rare; 35 minutes for medium; 45 minutes for well done. Time may vary, so test for doneness.

If more gravy is needed, add a little more wine to the pan.

Allow meat to stand for about 10 minutes before slicing.

YIELD: 12 TO 14 BUFFET SERVINGS

Plum Chicken

Tangy and tasty. From the kitchen of my daughter, Marsha Patinkin Schwartzman.

Preheat oven to 375°.

Place chicken in a deep baking dish.

In a saucepan, combine all the remaining ingredients and bring to a boil.

Pour over the chicken and bake for 60 minutes.

YIELD: 10 TO 16 SERVINGS

8	whole boneless breasts, cut in half
2	10-ounce jar plum preserves
2	tablespoons ketchup
3	teaspoons lemon peel
2	tablespoons fresh lemon juice
3	teaspoons white wine vinegar
½	teaspoon Tabasco sauce
2	teaspoons grated onion
1	teaspoon ground ginger
½	teaspoon pepper

Stuffed Chicken Breasts

This is an old favorite recipe, a hit with everyone. Friends and family asked why I had not included it in my *Jewish Family Cookbook*. So here it is.

6	whole skinless and boneless chicken breasts
2	6-ounce boxes Uncle Ben's Wild Rice Mix
¼	cup apricot marmalade
¾	cup white wine
½	cup light soy sauce
	Lawry's seasoned salt
	plain toothpicks

Preheat oven to 350°.

Wash and dry the chicken breasts. Season well with the Lawry's salt. Prepare the wild rice mix according to instructions on the package.

Place some wild rice on one half of a breast. Fold over the other half and fasten with toothpicks. Continue with the balance of the chicken. The rest of the rice will be served later with the chicken.

Combine the apricot marmalade, white wine, and soy sauce. Mix well.

Spray a baking pan with an olive oil spray and place the chicken breasts in the pan. Brush the chicken breasts generously with the sauce. Bake for 25 minutes and turn. Brush once again with the sauce, and continue baking for an additional 25 minutes, until well glazed. Spoon leftover sauce in pan over chicken when serving.

Remove the toothpicks, spoon a portion of rice onto a plate, and place the breast on the rice. Serve with a lovely green vegetable.

YIELD: 6 SERVINGS

Caraway Noodles

I have always been fond of the flavor of caraway seed, and nothing could be simpler and more tasty than a batch of cooked noodles flavored with caraway seed and butter. A wonderful complement to any dish.

Cook noodles according to package instructions and drain. Add the caraway seed and butter and season to taste with Lawry's salt. Toss until thoroughly blended.

This dish can be made in advance and reheated.

YIELD: 6 TO 8 SERVINGS

1   8-ounce package
     semi-broad noodles

¼   cup caraway seed

¼   pound butter or
     margarine

     Lawry's seasoned salt
     to taste

Strawberry-Applesauce Mold

I love the appearance of a Jell-O mold on a buffet table. This is a delicious salad. When unmolded, garnish with sliced strawberries and kiwi fruit. If possible, nestle some clean lemon or lime leaves in between.

1	6-ounce package strawberry Jell-O
1½	cups boiling water
1	1-pound package frozen sliced strawberries in juice (defrosted)
1	15-ounce jar applesauce
1	tablespoon fresh lemon juice

Dissolve Jell-O in boiling water. Add strawberries. Stir in applesauce and fresh lemon juice. Mix well.

Pour into a lightly greased 8- to 10-cup mold and refrigerate until firm. Unmold and garnish.

YIELD: 8 TO 10 SERVINGS

Passover

Passover

In our family, Passover has always been a happening. When we were younger, we all gathered at Auntie Ida's home for the first seder. The table was always set with "the red glass dishes" reserved for Pesach, and everyone gathered around the big table for the reading of the Haggadah, the story of the Jewish people's exodus from Egypt. Our hearts were filled with song, and sing we did. While we were, and are, blessed to be living in the land of freedom, we must never forget that there are those less fortunate and we remember them in our prayers.

A very important part of the seder, of course, is the traditional foods that are served. While many of the foods can be served during the course of the year, particular attention is paid to the preparation at Passover. No leavening of any kind is to be used; matzo is served instead of bread. Items that are purchased bear a mark that states these foods have been prepared according to Jewish law and may be eaten for Passover. Whether one is or is not very observant during the rest of the year, at Passover time we try to maintain the tradition.

The suggested menu is just a suggestion. Be creative.

Passover

Charoses-Horseradish-Matzo

Gefilte Fish and/or Mock Chopped Liver

Grandma Doralee's Chicken Soup with Matzo Balls

Eye of the Rib Roast
and/or Roasted Chicken with Veggies
and/or "Gedemfte" Chicken

Passover Tam Tam Kugel
and/or Passover Carrot Kugel

Roasted Portobello Mushrooms, Peppers, and Onions

Passover Nut Sponge Cake
Passover Almond-Orange Chocolate Cake
Passover Brownies
Mandelbrot Crust Cheesecake for Passover
Macaroon Lemon Tart for Passover
Passover Florentines
Butter Pecan Matzo Crisps

Fresh Fruit Platter

Charoses

This delicious concoction is one of the symbolic foods placed on the seder plate. Its meaning is described during the reading of the Haggadah on Passover. It is loved by everyone; huge quantities are always made to be eaten during the seder or, if there are any leftovers, during the week of Passover. There are many, many recipes for charoses. This is one of my family's recipes. By the way, before food processors arrived on the scene, we used an old-fashioned chopping bowl and metal chopper.

Preheat oven to 300° and toast the pecans for about 15 minutes. Watch so that they do not burn.

Core the apples and cut into chunks. Place all the ingredients in a food processor. Using the steel blade, pulse on and off. Do not let the mixture become watery. It should be "mildly coarse," resembling mortar, which it represents on the seder plate. Should you have a problem getting the right texture, add more ground nuts. By the way, *I* never use the honey.

YIELD: 24 SERVINGS. I SUGGEST DOUBLING THIS RECIPE!

12	*large Granny Smith apples*
3	*cups toasted ground pecans*
½	*cup Concord grape or Malaga wine*
1½	*tablespoons ground cinnamon*
½	*teaspoon ground cloves*
½	*teaspoon ground ginger*
⅓	*cup honey (for a sweeter flavor)*

Gefilte Fish

There's nothing like the aroma of gefilte fish cooking. Like it or not, it is very nostalgic. This is my version of a family recipe, changed just slightly. As a young child, I remember going to my grandma's house after the fish was cooked. She would save all the bones and my mother and I would sit in the kitchen and lick the bones clean.

If you live in a region where the following types of fish are not available, as I now do, substitute as best you can. It is delicious with fresh salmon. (Would you believe—pink gefilte fish?) Be sure to ask the fish market for the bones, if available. Bones add flavor, and help to congeal the sauce.

2	pounds whitefish
2	pounds trout
2	pounds pike
1	large onion, cut into chunks
2	carrots, grated
1	whole egg
1	6-ounce glass cold water
1	tablespoon sugar
	salt and pepper to taste
	fish bones
	sliced onions and carrots

In a food processor, using the steel blade, chop the fish until it is of a smooth consistency. Transfer to a large bowl. Process the onion and carrots and add to the fish. Beat the egg until frothy and add to the fish along with the water, sugar, salt, and pepper. Form into desired size balls.

Line your stockpot with the bones and sliced onions and carrots, and fill with water as you would for a soup. Bring to a boil. Place the fish balls in the pot very carefully. Reduce to medium heat and cook for about 1½ hours. Remove pot from heat and allow to cool. Lift fish balls out of the pot very carefully. Strain the broth and spoon over the fish when cool. Place in refrigerator until ready to serve.

Serve cold with red or white horseradish.

YIELD: AT LEAST 12 SERVINGS

Mock Chopped Liver

I love experimenting, and so I decided to try using mushrooms, as string beans and peas were not permissable for Passover. I think the result is delicious. Try it. I think you will be pleased.

In a deep skillet, heat the Nyafat or peanut oil. Add the onions and sauté slowly for at least 45 minutes. Add the mushrooms and walnuts and continue to cook for just a few minutes. The mushrooms should be crisp.

Place the Tam Tam crackers in a food processor. Add the mushroom mixture and salt and pepper. Process until you have the proper consistency. Add the boiled eggs. Do not overprocess. Adjust seasonings.

This may be molded or served in a beautiful bowl. Garnish with the chopped white of a boiled egg and sprinkle with finely chopped parsley.

Serve with Tam Tam crackers.

YIELD: 4 TO 6 SERVINGS

2 to 3 tablespoons Nyafat (available in the kosher food section of your local supermarket) or peanut oil

1½ very large sweet onions, sliced

½ pound fresh white mushrooms, cut into large pieces

½ cup walnuts

6 to 8 Tam Tam crackers (onion-garlic flavored), broken into pieces

½ teaspoon salt

¼ teaspoon white pepper

2 hard-boiled eggs (save a little of the whites–finely chopped–for garnish

finely chopped parsley for garnish

Grandma Doralee's Chicken Soup

Many doctors believe that chicken soup is a holistic form of penicillin. It's good for whatever ails you! The addition of chicken feet to the soup is wonderful. They are very important as so many of the nutrients we need are derived from the bones. When we were children, our mothers always made soup with the feet. They began to disappear from the stores years ago, but I recently discovered that the Asian markets always have them. Try your local Asian food market for the large soup chickens as well as the chicken feet. I purchase several packages at a time and keep them in the freezer.

1	large stewing chicken
1	package chicken feet (optional)
1	large onion, peeled and halved
12	large carrots, peeled and cut into chunks
6	celery ribs, cut into large pieces
1	bunch of parsley
1	teaspoon mild Hungarian paprika
1	teaspoon kosher salt
⅛	teaspoon white pepper

Place the chicken in a very large stockpot with enough water to cover. Bring to a hard boil and skim off the top. Add the vegetables, paprika, salt, and pepper. Bring to a boil once again and then reduce to a low heat and cook for about 3 hours.

Remove the chicken and vegetables, saving the carrots, and strain the soup. In order to remove the fat, I suggest using a gravy separator or placing the soup in the freezer for a short while, allowing the fat to rise. Serve with the carrots and matzo balls.

YIELD: 10 TO 12 SERVINGS

Matzo Balls

Another version of knaidlach, different from the one in my first book. These are great. The club soda keeps them light and fluffy.

With a whisk, lightly blend the eggs, olive oil, and soda. Add the balance of the ingredients, except the soup powder, and whisk just until blended. Place mixture in refrigerator for 30 minutes.

Fill a stockpot with water. Add the instant chicken soup powder and bring to a boil. Make balls about the size of golf balls and place gently in the hot liquid. Cover, reduce to moderate heat, and cook gently for 45 minutes. Remove from heat and allow matzo balls to cool in liquid. Remove gently. When ready to serve, drop matzo balls into hot chicken soup and simmer for at least an hour.

YIELD: 12 TO 18 MATZO BALLS

4	large eggs
3	tablespoons olive oil
½	cup club soda
1	cup matzo meal
½	teaspoon salt
⅛	teaspoon white pepper
¼	teaspoon garlic powder
1	tablespoon chopped fresh parsley
2	tablespoons instant chicken soup powder

Eye of the Rib Roast

As far as I'm concerned, there is still nothing better than a beef roast for dinner. However, I usually consult my guests when I am planning a menu today to see whether this will be acceptable. With a few exceptions, it usually is. I usually figure 18 to 20 minutes per pound for rare roast beef. If you prefer, use a meat thermometer.

1   *eye of the rib roast*
Lawry's seasoned salt
ground black pepper
caraway seed
½   *cup chili sauce*
1   *cup red wine (your favorite table wine)*

Preheat oven to 450°.

Wash and dry the meat. Season it well with seasoned salt and black pepper and pat on lots of caraway seed. Frost the roast with the chili sauce. Add the 1 cup red wine to the pan.

Place in a roasting pan and roast uncovered for 30 minutes. Reduce heat to 350°. Baste your roast with the wine gravy. Insert your meat thermometer and continue to roast until you have reached your preference, rare, medium, or well done.

When meat has reached desired doneness, remove from pan to cutting board and allow it to cool for at least 10 minutes.

YIELD: FIGURE ½ POUND PER PERSON

Roasted Chicken and Veggies

The succulence of the chicken, flavored with wine, seasonings, vegetables, and dried cherries, makes this a gourmet delight.

Preheat oven to 375°.

Spray a large roasting pan or oven-to-table baking dish with vegetable spray. Season chicken well with poultry seasoning and Lawry's salt. Place in baking pan and arrange vegetables around the chicken. Sprinkle dried cherries around. Combine the olive oil with the wine and pour over the chicken. Cover tightly and bake for 1 hour. Remove cover, baste with gravy, and bake for an additional 30 minutes, or until tender.

YIELD: 4 TO 5 SERVINGS

1	whole large roasting chicken
	poultry seasoning
	Lawry's seasoned salt
1	pound packaged small peeled carrots
8 to 10	garlic cloves
8	sun-dried tomato halves, cut into small pieces
1	large onion, cut into pieces
6	medium-size red potatoes, scrubbed and cut into quarters
½	cup dried pitted tart cherries
⅛	cup olive oil
½	cup chardonnay wine

"Gedemfte" Chicken

This is a slightly updated version of a marvelous old-fashioned dish. It is always a winner. Be sure to make enough so that you have leftovers—they are wonderful the next day. By the way, *gedemfte* means "potted."

1	very large onion, cut into small chunks
2	cups unseasoned Italian tomato sauce
1	cup fine red wine
3	garlic cloves, chopped
2	small bay leaves
1	teaspoon Lawry's seasoned salt
½	teaspoon white pepper
½	teaspoon dried basil
¼	teaspoon rosemary
½	teaspoon curry powder
8	pieces skinless chicken (bone in), white or dark meat
2	pounds medium-size baby carrots
6	russet potatoes, cut into 2-inch slices

In a very large Dutch oven, combine all ingredients, except chicken, carrots, and potatoes. Bring to a boil and reduce to a simmer. Place the chicken, carrots, and potatoes in the sauce. Cook over low heat for at least 2½ hours, basting occasionally, so that potatoes and carrots are covered with sauce. Taste while cooking to adjust seasonings.

YIELD: 6 TO 8 SERVINGS

Passover Tam Tam Kugel

I decided to try to make something different with flavored Tam Tams, which recently appeared for Passover. This is much lighter than the usual matzo kugel. It can also be used as a stuffing.

Preheat oven to 350°.

Using the steel blade of a food processor, chop the carrots, celery, and onion together. Process the mushrooms separately and set aside. In a medium skillet, heat the Nyafat and sauté the carrots, celery, and onion. When almost done, add the mushrooms and continue to cook for just a few more minutes.

Place the crackers and mushroom mixture in the food processor. Add the eggs, butter or margarine, and seasonings. Process well.

Turn into a greased oven-to-table casserole so that kugel will be about 2 inches high. Bake for 30 minutes (or more), until the top is nice and crusty.

YIELD: 10 TO 12 SERVINGS

2	large carrots
4	celery ribs
1	medium onion
1	pound fresh mushrooms
2	tablespoons Nyafat (available in the kosher food section of your local supermarket)
1	box Tam Tam Passover crackers (onion-garlic flavored)
2	extra-large eggs
¼	pound butter or margarine, melted
½	teaspoon salt
¼	teaspoon white pepper
1	teaspoon mild Hungarian paprika
¼	teaspoon garlic powder

Passover Carrot Kugel

This is an old family favorite, served not only at almost every holiday meal, but also at any time during the year. While this recipe appeared in *Grandma Doralee Patinkin's Jewish Family Cookbook,* I have included it again, as the children love it. However, this version differs from the Carrot Kugel served during the year, as a Passover recipe contains no leavening of any kind. It will not be quite as light, but still just as delicious.

¾	cup cake meal
¾	cup potato starch
½	teaspoon salt
½	teaspoon cinnamon
½	teaspoon nutmeg
¼	teaspoon ground cloves
¼	pound butter or margarine
½	cup oil
½	cup brown sugar
2	egg yolks
1¾	cups grated carrots
¼	cup fresh lemon juice
	grated rind of 1 lemon
3	egg whites

Sift the cake meal, potato starch, salt, and spices together. Combine margarine, oil, brown sugar, and egg yolks in a food processor. Blend well. Add the carrots and lemon juice and rind and blend once again. Incorporate the dry ingredients. Remove batter to a large bowl. Beat the egg whites until stiff and fold into the batter.

Pour into a 4½-cup greased ring mold or an 8½ x 11-inch baking pan. Place in refrigerator overnight. Remove from refrigerator and allow to stand at room temperature for ½ hour prior to baking. Preheat oven to 350°.

Bake for 45 to 60 minutes. Test with a toothpick at 45 minutes.

This may be frozen unbaked. When ready to bake, remove from freezer and allow to stand at room temperature for about 1 hour before baking. It may be necessary to allow additional time for baking if not thawed completely.

YIELD: 10 TO 12 SERVINGS

Roasted Portobello Mushrooms, Peppers, and Onions

These are a wonderful addition to any type of meal. I also love them on a grilled onion roll.

Marinate the vegetables in the sauce or marinade for at least 1 hour.

If grilling, use a basket and grill for 2 to 3 minutes on each side, or just until tender. Do not overcook. If roasting, spray your roasting sheet with an olive oil mister before placing the vegetables on it. Preheat oven to 400° and roast 15 to 20 minutes, turning once.

YIELD: WILL DEPEND UPON AMOUNT OF VEGETABLES USED.

portobello mushrooms, trimmed, and cut into ¾-inch strips

your favorite marinade or teriyaki sauce

red bell peppers, cut into ½-inch strips

sweet onions, sliced

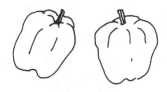

Passover Nut Sponge Cake

This delicious cake was one of Mandy's favorites when he was a boy. It is especially good served with a fruit sauce and lots of whipped cream or dairy topping. However, I'm sorry to say that the younger cooks of today are forsaking the traditional Passover desserts in favor of something different.

½	cup cake meal
¼	cup potato starch
½	teaspoon salt
½	cup ground pecans
8	jumbo-size eggs, at room temperature, separated
1⅓	cups sugar
	grated rind of 1 navel orange
⅓	cup orange juice or half orange and half lemon juice

Preheat oven to 325°.

Sift the cake meal, potato starch, and salt. Add the nuts, mix well, and set aside.

Using your electric mixer, beat yolks until thick. Add half of the sugar, the rind, and juice. Continue beating until thick and fluffy. Fold in dry ingredients.

In a separate bowl, beat egg whites and a pinch of salt until foamy. Add the balance of sugar gradually. Beat until stiff peaks form.

Fold egg yolk mixture into egg whites.

Pour into ungreased 10-inch tube pan with a removable bottom. Plunge a spatula or fork around the batter several times to equalize it.

Bake on the low rack of the oven for 40 minutes. Increase temperature to 350° and bake for 15 or 20 minutes longer. Test with a toothpick; if it comes out clean, your cake is ready to remove from the oven.

Invert for several hours to cool and stretch.

YIELD: 10 TO 12 SERVINGS

Passover Almond-Orange Chocolate Cake

This is another version of a marvelous Passover sponge cake.

½   cup sliced almonds

7   jumbo-size eggs, at room temperature, separated

1¼   cups sugar

1   tablespoon orange juice

½   teaspoon freshly grated orange peel

⅓   cup potato starch

¼   cup cake meal

⅓   cup Droste's cocoa

¼   teaspoon salt

Preheat oven to 300°.

Toast almonds in a flat pan; cool completely. Place sliced almonds in food processor bowl; process to a fine grind.

Using an electric mixer, beat egg yolks in a large bowl until lemon colored. Gradually add 1 cup sugar, beating until thick. Stir in juice and orange peel. Sift together potato starch, cake meal, and cocoa; fold into yolk mixture. Fold in ground almonds.

Again, using the electric mixer, beat egg whites and salt in a separate large bowl until foamy. Gradually add remaining ¼ cup sugar in small amounts, beating until stiff peaks form. Gently fold about 1 cup egg white mixture into yolk mixture. Fold all of yolk mixture into remaining whites.

Pour into ungreased 9- or 10-inch tube pan. Bake for 30 minutes. Without opening oven door, increase oven temperature to 325°. Bake for 15 minutes, or until top springs back when touched lightly.

Invert on heatproof funnel or bottle. When completely cool, remove from pan.

YIELD: 10 TO 12 SERVINGS

Passover Brownies

This is always a winner. People just love brownies. This differs from the brownie made during the year because there is no leavening. I always beat the egg whites when using the cake meal and potato starch.

Preheat oven to 350°.

Beat the egg whites until stiff and set aside.

Melt the chocolate and the butter or margarine (in a large glass bowl in your microwave, if you have one).

Add the sugar, egg yolks, and vanilla to the chocolate mixture. Sift the cake meal and potato starch together and add to the chocolate mixture. Add the grated orange rind and the chopped nuts. Fold in the stiffly beaten egg whites.

Pour into a greased 9-inch square pan and bake for 20 to 25 minutes.

Remove from oven and cool on a cake rack. Cut into desired sizes.

YIELD: 16 TO 20 SERVINGS

2	jumbo-size eggs, at room temperature, separated
2	ounces unsweetened baking chocolate
¼	pound butter or margarine
1	cup sugar
1	teaspoon vanilla extract
¼	cup cake meal
¼	cup potato starch
1	teaspoon grated orange rind
⅓	cup chopped nuts

Mandelbrot-Crust Cheesecake for Passover

As I have always said, is there a cheesecake I do not like? This is just a simple and easy version, suitable for Passover.

CRUST

3   cups Passover man-
    delbrot crumbs

2   teaspoons cinnamon

1   cup toasted chopped
    pecans

6   tablespoons butter,
    melted

FILLING

4   8-ounce packages
    cream cheese

1⅓ cups sugar

3   teaspoons vanilla
    extract

    grated rind and juice
    of 2 lemons

4   whole eggs

GARNISH

    sliced fresh straw-
    berries

    frozen sliced straw-
    berries in syrup
    (optional)

Preheat oven to 350°.

Mix crumbs and butter and press into a 9- or 10-inch springform pan.

Combine cheese, sugar, vanilla, and lemon juice. Blend until smooth. Add eggs, one at a time, blending well after each one. Add the grated rind.

Pour over the crust. Bake for 55 to 60 minutes, or until center is almost set. Remove from oven and cool on a cake rack.

Refrigerate until ready to serve. Garnish with sliced fresh strawberries placed around and in the center of the cake. Top with a spoonful of frozen sliced berries in syrup if you want.

YIELD: AT LEAST 12 SERVINGS

Macaroon Lemon Tart for Passover

A tart lemony dessert after a seder meal is delightful. This is so simple and so good!

Preheat oven to 350°.

Mix crumbs and butter and press into an 8-inch tart pan. Bake the crust for 15 minutes and remove from oven.

Place all the filling ingredients, except the butter and almonds, in a saucepan or double boiler. Blend well with a whisk. Place over low heat and cook, stirring constantly with a wooden spoon, until mixture thickens. As it comes to a boil, remove from heat. Add butter and cool. Spoon into tart pan. Garnish with toasted almonds. Refrigerate for several hours.

YIELD: 6 TO 8 SERVINGS

CRUST

3	cups macaroon crumbs (any flavor)
4	tablespoons butter, melted

FILLING

2	jumbo-size eggs
½	cup sugar
⅓	cup fresh lemon juice
2	teaspoons grated fresh lemon rind
¼	pound butter, at room temperature
1	cup toasted sliced almonds

Passover Florentines

There is no flour in this recipe—only Passover cake meal. These don't last very long. They just disappear. Many recipes used during the year can easily be adapted for Passover, so experiment.

2½	cups sliced almonds
1	cup sugar
¼	pound butter, melted
5	tablespoons cake meal
2	egg whites, slightly beaten
	dash of salt
½	teaspoon vanilla extract

Preheat oven to 350°. Line cookie sheets with baking parchment.

Toss almonds and sugar together. Stir in melted butter. Stir in cake meal, egg whites, salt, and vanilla. Stir until well blended.

Drop by spoonfuls about 2 inches apart onto cookie sheets.

Bake one sheet at a time for 10 minutes, or until golden brown around the edges and bottom. Cool on the parchment.

Option: When cool, brush one end of each cookie with melted semisweet chocolate. Place on waxed paper and allow to harden.

YIELD: AT LEAST 36 COOKIES

Butter Pecan Matzo Crisps

Fate smiled upon me, when I recently met Edie Greenberg. This is just one of many of her wonderful recipes. It is a marvelous candy for Passover.

Preheat oven to 375°.

Lay 2 of the matzos side by side in a 10 x 15-inch rimmed baking pan lined with aluminum foil. Break the other matzo and fill in along the side and the top.

In a 1½- to 2-quart pan, melt the butter over medium heat. Add sugar and pecans and stir often until mixture comes to a rolling boil, then boil until big shiny bubbles form—about 1 to 2 minutes.

Remove from heat, stir in vanilla, and immediately pour hot mixture over matzos. Spread sugar mixture quickly and evenly, with back of spoon or spatula, up to but not over edges of matzos.

Transfer pan to oven and bake until matzos are a little crisp, about 3 to 6 minutes. While matzos are baking, melt the chocolate and cream in a double boiler or in the microwave oven. Mix until smooth.

Remove matzos from oven and spread with melted chocolate. Let cool until chocolate hardens. Break into small pieces.

YIELD: AT LEAST 12 TO 18 PIECES

3	unsalted matzos, each 6 inches square (I prefer Thin Tea Matzos)
1	cup butter or margarine
1	cup firmly packed brown sugar
1	cup pecan pieces
1	teaspoon vanilla
1	cup semi-sweet chocolate chips
¼	cup cream or milk

Fresh Fruit Platter

When I do not want to make a cut-up salad, I slice the fruit into wide pieces and arrange by color on an attractive serving platter. If you can obtain some lemon or lime leaves, wash them carefully and dry them. Place them around the edge of the platter and cluster the fruit on them, allowing the leaves to show.

melons of choice
fresh pineapple
strawberries
blueberries
papaya
almost any fruit that will remain firm when cut

A platter can be arranged in advance and covered with plastic wrap and placed in the refrigerator.

YIELD: FIGURE ABOUT 1 CUP PER PERSON

Bridal Luncheon

Bridal Luncheon

As our children and my friends' children were getting married, there were many showers and luncheons, some in hotels, some at home. The parties given at home were always wonderful, and I thought I would share my memories with you. Sometimes the affair might be a brunch or sometimes a lunch, but always simple and tasty.

Always use fresh flowers for centerpieces, in keeping with the season, and try to establish a color scheme and carry it throughout the party.

Remember, things are not as formal as they once were. There are lovely paper and plastic party goods available. Used with some of your beautiful china and crystal serving pieces, it can be just smashing.

Bridal Luncheon

Split Pea-Tomato Bisque
with Toasted Pita Chips

Fresh Salmon Cakes
and/or
Hot Chicken Salad

Rice with Peas and Mushrooms

Grapefruit-Orange-Jicama-Sweet Onion Salad
Strawberry or Raspberry Dressing

Orange Crescent Rolls
or
Miniature Buttermilk Cheese Biscuits

Ice Cream-Filled Cream Puffs
with Raspberry Sauce
or Kahlúa Mud Pie

Split Pea—Tomato Bisque

I love to serve this with toasted pita chips as a preamble to lunch or dinner. Smooth and elegant.

In a deep saucepan, blend the two soups well with the water and white wine. Stir over medium heat.

YIELD: 4 TO 6 SERVINGS

1	10½-ounce can vegetarian split pea soup (undiluted)
1	10½-ounce can tomato soup (undiluted)
½	cup water
1	cup dry white wine

Toasted Pita Chips

These can be made ahead, stored in an airtight container, and heated again when ready to serve. They are marvelous with soups as well as dips.

Preheat oven to 325°.

Place pita wedges on a large baking sheet. Brush generously with olive oil and sprinkle generously with Parmesan cheese. Sprinkle with paprika. Bake until crisp, 15 to 20 minutes.

packaged pita bread (small size), cut into wedges
olive oil
Parmesan cheese
mild Hungarian paprika

Fresh Salmon Cakes

The fresh salmon makes these absolutely wonderful, and nothing like the old-fashioned salmon patties that we used to make. These are more like crab cakes.

1	pound fresh poached salmon
3	cups fresh bread crumbs
2	cups diced fresh plum tomatoes
3	eggs
½	cup minced shallots
2	tablespoons Dijon mustard
¼	cup chopped chives
¼	cup chopped celery
1	tablespoon dried mustard
	salt and pepper to taste
	peanut oil for frying

In a large bowl or food processor, mix the salmon with 1 cup of the bread crumbs and the remaining ingredients. Blend well. Form into desired size cakes and roll in the remaining 2 cups bread crumbs.

Using a rather deep skillet, heat the oil and place the salmon cakes in the hot oil. Fry until crisp on both sides. Remove from oil and place on paper towels for just a few seconds to remove excess oil. Serve while hot.

YIELD: 6 TO 8 SERVINGS

Hot Chicken Salad

This was always a favorite at the bridal luncheons. I also use it for brunches, and it is always a winner. Thanks again, Aunt Ethel.

Preheat oven to 350°.

Thoroughly combine all the salad ingredients and put in a casserole.

Blend the topping ingredients and scatter over the salad.

Bake uncovered for 25 minutes. Serve while hot.

YIELD: 8 SERVINGS

3	pounds cooked boneless, skinless breasts of chicken, cut into bite-size pieces
1	cup chopped celery
6	green onions, sliced on the diagonal very fine
1	small can pitted ripe olives
1	cup small stuffed green olives
1	cup mayonnaise
1	tablespoon Worcestershire sauce
½	teaspoon salt
¼	teaspoon white pepper
¼	teaspoon curry powder

TOPPING

1	cup cornflake crumbs
½	teaspoon garlic powder
2	tablespoons butter, melted

Rice with Peas and Mushrooms

This dish is a nice complement to almost any entrée; however I especially enjoy serving this with my Hot Chicken Salad (see previous recipe). The salad could be served alongside or over the rice.

2	cups long-grain white rice, cooked according to package instructions (for best results, use the microwave method)
2	cups frozen peas
2	cups sliced white mushrooms, sautéed in 2 tablespoons butter
¼	teaspoon Lawry's seasoned salt
⅛	teaspoon white pepper

Combine all the ingredients. Place in an oven-to-table casserole and heat thoroughly (in microwave) when ready to serve.

YIELD: 8 TO 10 SERVINGS

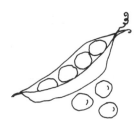

Grapefruit-Orange-Jicama-Sweet Onion Salad

This is a delightful summer salad. The combination of flavors is wonderful! Sprinkle with my Strawberry or Raspberry Salad Dressing.

Combine all the ingredients, except pine nuts, and toss gently. When ready to serve, plate individually, sprinkle with the salad dressing, and top with some toasted pine nuts.

YIELD: 4 TO 6 SERVINGS

2   navel oranges, peeled and sliced

2   cups grapefruit sections (available in jars in produce section)

1   medium-size sweet white or red onion, sliced very thin

1   small jicama, cut into narrow strips

2   cups romaine lettuce cut into bite-size pieces

1   cup spring greens
toasted pine nuts

Strawberry or Raspberry Salad Dressing

This is a delicious fruit dressing. Serve over a spinach salad with strawberries, jicama, and slivered green onions, or with my Grapefruit-Orange-Jicama-Sweet Onion Salad. When fresh fruits are in season, combine them with spring greens and some buttered lettuce and use this dressing.

1	cup fresh strawberries or raspberries
2	tablespoons strawberry or raspberry preserves
1 to 2	teaspoons Dijon mustard
¼	teaspoon powdered ginger
½	cup raspberry vinegar or rice vinegar
¼	cup oil

Blend all the ingredients in a food processor or blender. Chill before serving.

YIELD: 1½ CUPS

Orange Crescent Rolls

A delightful little morsel, and so easy to make.

Preheat oven to 375°.

Open package and roll out the 8 triangles. Cut each triangle in half.

Place the rolls point side away from you. Spread each triangle with a little orange marmalade. Roll from the wide edge down to the point.

Place on a greased cookie sheet. Brush with beaten egg or melted butter.

Bake for 11 to 13 minutes, or until golden brown.

YIELD: 16 ROLLS

1	*package crescent dinner rolls*
	orange marmalade (regular or sugar free)

Miniature Buttermilk Cheese Biscuits

Hot biscuits are always a winner. The cheese adds a special kick. Use mild or sharp cheese, whichever you prefer.

2	cups flour
4	teaspoons baking powder
1	teaspoon salt
2	tablespoons butter
¾	cup shredded Cheddar cheese
½	teaspoon baking soda
1	cup buttermilk

Preheat oven to 400°.

Sift together the flour, baking powder, and salt. Add the butter and shredded cheese and blend into the flour until a little mealy.

Add the baking soda to the buttermilk and stir.

Combine the buttermilk mixture with the flour mixture. Blend well, but do not overbeat. Drop by spoonfuls into greased mini muffin pans. Bake for 12 to 15 minutes.

Serve hot, or warm in the toaster oven.

YIELD: 12 TO 18 MUFFINS

Ice Cream—Filled Cream Puffs

In my younger days I often served these. Of course, they were always a hit with young and old. The puffs can be made a day ahead and stored in an airtight container. Serve with Raspberry Sauce (see page 79).

Preheat oven to 450°.

Add the butter to the boiling water. Stir with a wooden spoon until butter melts. Add flour and salt all at once. Stir the mixture vigorously. Cook, stirring constantly, until the dough pulls away from the sides of the pan and forms a ball around the spoon. Remove from heat and cool slightly.

Add the eggs, one at a time, beating until smooth after each.

For miniature puffs, drop by a tablespoon about 2 inches apart onto a parchment-covered baking sheet. Bake for 10 minutes. Reduce oven heat to 325° and bake for an additional 15 to 20 minutes. Watch carefully. Cool on wire rack.

When ready to serve, cut off tops and crisp up tops and bottoms in a 350° oven for just a few minutes. Fill with your favorite ice cream and plate with my raspberry sauce.

YIELD: 24 MINIATURE PUFFS

¼	pound butter
1	cup boiling water
1	cup sifted flour
⅓	teaspoon salt
4	eggs
	your favorite ice cream

Kahlúa Mud Pie

A crowd pleaser if there ever was one. Fill with your favorite chocolate or coffee ice cream, top it with whipped cream and enjoy!

16 to 20 chocolate ice cream wafers
2 quarts coffee or chocolate ice cream (softened)
½ cup Kahlúa liqueur
½ pint whipped cream

Line the bottom of a 10-inch deep-dish pie plate with half of the ice cream wafers. Sprinkle some Kahlúa over the wafers. Spread one quart of the ice cream over the wafers. Add another layer of chocolate wafers, sprinkle with more Kahlúa, and top with the balance of the ice cream. Place in freezer until ice cream is firm to the touch.

Cover with plastic wrap and then aluminum foil, and return to freezer.

When ready to serve, remove at least 25 minutes before serving. Top with the whipped cream and go to town!

YIELD: 8 TO 10 SERVINGS

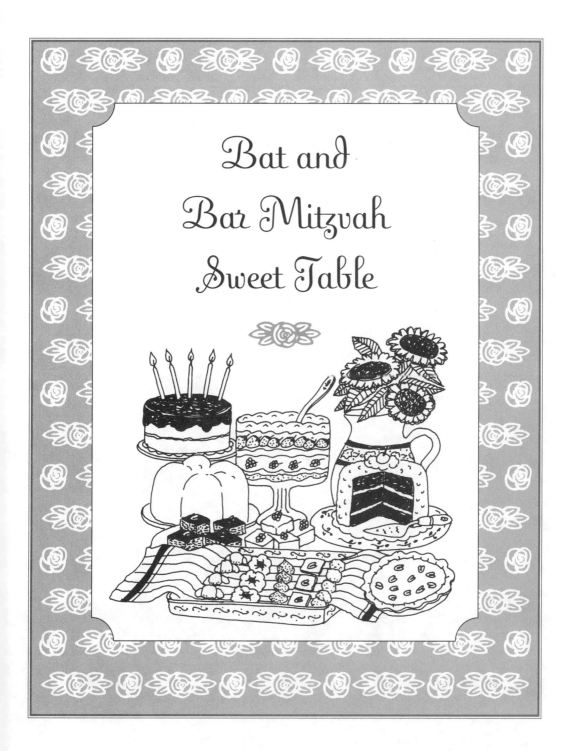

Bat and Bar Mitzvah Sweet Table

Bat and Bar Mitzvah Sweet Table

I have always said, "have cookies, will travel"—and travel I did. My suitcases filled with pastries traveled to Chicago, Reno, New York, and San Diego. Having fourteen grandchildren, I have had a world of experience in packing cookies for travel.

With the exception of a few items, most cookies and cakes travel well if packed correctly. The secret is lots of shoe boxes, coffee cans, waxed paper, aluminum foil, and paper towels. If packed tightly, they will not break. All containers are then placed in suitcases or cartons and secured with crumpled newspaper so that they do not move within the carton or suitcase. I always breathe a sigh of relief as my luggage appears on the carousel at the airport.

There are a few items that have to be refrigerated or do not travel well. I try to delegate these items to someone living near the celebrant.

Many of my favorite recipes appeared in my first book, *Grandma Doralee Patinkin's Jewish Family Cookbook*. Because my sweet tables present what I have been up to the last seventeen years, when our first granddaughter celebrated her Bat Mitzvah, I wanted to share with you some other special treats.

I am not usually involved with the setting up of the "sweet table," as I usually leave that to the caterer my children hire. However, I make my wishes known in advance, and it is usually very lovely.

I think if I had to choose a favorite chapter of either of my books, this would probably be the most exciting for me. Planning and baking, which usually involves some of my close friends and daughters Marsha and Joanne, and then packing carefully for that very special day is a wonderfully rewarding experience for a grandmother.

Just remember, when loving hands are involved in the preparation, and you follow the recipes carefully, your dessert tables will be as lovely as mine have always been.

Sweet Table Selections

Almond Jam Bars

Blonde Brownies

Grandma Doralee's Butter Crisps

Cheesecake Squares

Chocolate Chunky Nutty

Chocolate Kisses

Grandma Doralee's Coffee Brownies

Grandma Doralee's Double Chocolate Brownies

Grandma Doralee's Brownies

Graham Cracker Pralines

Miniature Cream Puffs with
Chocolate Mousse or Lemon Filling

Doralee's Triple-Threat Delights

Rugelach

Chocolate-Kahlúa Pecan Tart

Turtle Pecan Cheesecake

Cognac Brownies

Marsha's Trifle

Almond Jam Bars

This was one of Papa Lester's favorites.

2	cups sifted flour
½	pound butter
½	cup sugar
⅛	teaspoon salt
1	egg yolk
½	cup raspberry preserves
⅓	cup sliced natural almonds
½	teaspoon almond extract

Preheat oven to 350°.

Combine the flour, butter, sugar, salt, and egg yolk and process until mealy. Form into 3 balls. Shape each ball by hand into a 12 x 1-inch roll. Place on a parchment-covered cookie sheet about 4 inches apart. With back of teaspoon, make a lengthwise depression about ½ inch deep down center of each roll.

Combine the raspberry preserves with the sliced almonds and almond extract.

Spread a small amount of preserves and almonds into the depression. Do not overfill. Place additional almonds in a row over the filling.

Bake for 25 minutes, or until light golden brown.

Cool slightly. Cut strips diagonally into desired size.

YIELD: 24 TO 36 PIECES

Blonde Brownies

I recently lunched at Delicias in Rancho Santa Fe, California (it is a must if you are in the area). Accompanying a delicious, very light sorbet was this extravagantly rich cookie. Their pastry chef, Elizabeth E. Harris, was gracious enough to send me the recipe. These are to die for.

Preheat oven to 350°.

Combine flour, salt, and baking powder in a bowl. Set aside. In a processor or electric mixer, beat butter and sugar until light and fluffy. Beat in eggs, one at a time. Add vanilla. Add flour mixture until just incorporated. Add the nuts and white chocolate chunks.

Grease and lightly flour a 9 x 13-inch pan. Pour batter into pan and spread evenly. Bake for 25 to 30 minutes. Remove from oven and allow to cool before cutting. Cut into narrow bars.

YIELD: 24 TO 36 PIECES

2	cups flour
½	teaspoon salt
1¼	teaspoons baking powder
½	pound softened butter
2	cups brown sugar
3	whole eggs
2	teaspoons vanilla extract
1	cup coarsely chopped macadamia nuts
1	cup coarsely chopped white chocolate

Grandma Doralee's Butter Crisps

This has become my signature cookie, so it had to be repeated from my previous book. It is everyone's favorite, especially my grandchildren. If Grandma is coming, so are the butter crisps.

2¼ cups flour

1   cup sifted powdered sugar

½   teaspoon salt

½   pound butter, or half butter half margarine

1   egg, beaten until light

2   teaspoons vanilla extract

1   egg white, slightly beaten with 1 tablespoon water

cinnamon and sugar

Place flour, sugar, salt, and butter in a food processor. Using steel blade, blend until mealy. Sprinkle 2 tablespoons of the beaten egg and the vanilla over the mixture in processor and process until mixture forms a ball.

Remove dough from processor and shape into 5 long rolls about 1¼ inches in diameter. Wrap in waxed paper, place on a cookie sheet, and place in freezer. When frozen, place rolls in a plastic bag and store in freezer until you are ready to bake them. Should you want to bake them instead of storing them for later, they should be frozen slightly in order to slice easily.

When ready to bake: Preheat oven to 400°. Slice dough about ¼ inch thick, brush with beaten egg white, sprinkle with cinnamon and sugar, and place on cookie sheet covered with baking parchment. These cookies burn very rapidly, which is why I suggest using parchment.

Bake for 5 to 10 minutes. Allow to cool on parchment and store in airtight container.

YIELD: 80 TO 90 CRISPS

Cheesecake Squares

Scrumptious! Delicious! Always a favorite on the dessert table. This is very rich, so cut them into small pieces. Note: I usually make the cookie dough and topping ahead and store in the refrigerator.

Blend all cookie dough ingredients. Place on a flat surface and knead into a ball. Divide into 2 portions. Wrap in waxed paper or plastic wrap and refrigerate. This can also be frozen.

Preheat oven to 350°.

Use one half of the cookie dough and press into a 7 x 11-inch Pyrex baking dish. Bake for 25 minutes, or until lightly browned.

Combine the filling ingredients and pour over the baked crust.

Combine the topping ingredients and sprinkle over the cheese filling.

Bake for another 25 minutes. Cool and cut into desired size.

This cookie freezes well.

YIELD: 24 SQUARES

BUTTER COOKIE DOUGH

2½	cups sifted flour
½	pound butter
½	cup sugar
1	large egg
1	teaspoon vanilla extract

FILLING

1	8-ounce package cream cheese
¼	cup sugar
1	whole egg
2	tablespoons sour cream
1	tablespoon lemon juice
½	teaspoon vanilla extract

TOPPING

¼	cup brown sugar
2	tablespoons flour
1	tablespoon butter
½	teaspoon cinnamon
½	cup chopped nuts

Chocolate Chunky Nutty

I tasted this cookie many years ago at a family party and have loved it ever since. If you like a chewy morsel, this is it.

6	ounces semisweet chocolate
4	ounces unsweetened baking chocolate
¼	pound butter
1¼	cups sugar
3	eggs
2	teaspoons vanilla extract
1	cup flour
1	teaspoon baking powder
¼	teaspoon salt
2	cups coarsely chopped toasted walnuts

Preheat oven to 325°.

Melt semisweet and unsweetened chocolate and butter. Add the sugar, eggs, and vanilla and blend thoroughly. Stir in the flour, baking powder, and salt. Add the nuts and blend.

On a parchment-covered cookie sheet, drop by heaping teaspoonfuls about 1 inch apart.

Bake for 12 minutes, no longer. Cool thoroughly and remove from cookie sheet.

YIELD: 60 COOKIES

Chocolate Kisses

The first time I made these must have been at least fifty years ago. They taste just like candy. From the kitchen of Auntie Ida.

Preheat oven to 350°.

Beat egg whites until foamy. Add the salt and gradually add the sugar. Beat until stiff and peaky.

Beat melted chocolate until smooth. (Beating will cool chocolate.) Add vanilla. Fold into egg white mixture. Add coconut.

Drop by teaspoonfuls onto a cookie sheet lined with baking parchment. Place in the preheated oven. Turn off the oven and allow them to remain in the oven overnight.

These should not be frozen, but can be stored in an airtight canister for several days.

YIELD: 36 PIECES

2	egg whites
¼	teaspoon salt
½	cup sugar
1½	cups semisweet chocolate chips, melted
½	teaspoon vanilla extract
1	cup shredded coconut

Grandma Doralee's Coffee Brownies

For those of us who like anything flavored with coffee, try serving these cut into large squares accompanied by coffee ice cream. You can't beat it!

1	cup flour
1	teaspoon baking powder
½	teaspoon salt
½	pound butter
3	ounces unsweetened baking chocolate
1	ounce bittersweet baking chocolate
4	extra large eggs
2	cups sugar
2	teaspoons vanilla extract
3	tablespoons instant espresso powder
2	tablespoons coffee-flavored liqueur (I prefer Kahlúa.)

Preheat oven to 350°.

Sift the flour, baking powder, and salt together and set aside.

Melt the butter and both chocolates. Stir until smooth. Set aside.

In your processor or electric mixer, beat the eggs, sugar, vanilla, espresso powder, and liqueur until mixture is thick and fluffy. Add the chocolate mixture and blend well. Add the flour mixture and blend only until incorporated.

Grease and lightly flour a 9 x 13-inch pan. Pour batter into pan and spread evenly.

Bake for 30 minutes. If you like a drier brownie, bake a little longer.

Remove from oven and cool completely before cutting. Dust lightly with powdered sugar if serving without ice cream.

YIELD: 24 TO 30 PIECES

Grandma Doralee's
Double Chocolate Brownies

Who doesn't like brownies? In this version of "my" brownie, I use two different kinds of chocolate and toasted walnuts and pecans. Rich, fudgy, and nutty. This is so fast and simple to make that I don't even bother to use a processor or mixer.

Preheat oven to 350°.

Melt the butter and chocolate in a large bowl. Stir until smooth. Add the eggs, sugar, and vanilla. Mix well. Add the flour, salt, and nuts. Blend well.

Grease and lightly flour a jelly-roll type pan, 11½ x 16½ inches. Pour batter into pan and spread evenly. Bake for 25 to 30 minutes. Test for doneness. Remove and completely cool before cutting.

YIELD: 36 TO 48 BROWNIES

1	*pound butter*
4	*ounces unsweetened baking chocolate*
4	*ounces bittersweet baking chocolate*
8	*extra large eggs*
4	*cups sugar*
4	*teaspoons vanilla*
2	*cups flour*
1	*teaspoon salt*
1	*cup toasted chopped walnuts*
1	*cup toasted chopped pecans*

Grandma Doralee's Brownies

While this recipe appeared in my *Jewish Family Cookbook*, I felt it had to be repeated, as this basic recipe is probably fifty to seventy-five years old. It is always in demand and you will always be pleased.

½	pound butter
4	squares unsweetened baking chocolate
4	whole eggs
2	cups sugar
2	teaspoons vanilla extract
1	cup flour
1	cup chopped nuts (optional)

Preheat oven to 350°.

Melt the chocolate and butter in a large bowl. Add the eggs, sugar, vanilla, flour, and nuts, if using. Blend well.

Pour into a well-greased and lightly floured pan, approximately 11 x 13 inches. Bake for 20 to 25 minutes. Remove from oven. Cool and cut into desired size.

YIELD: 24 TO 36 BROWNIES

Note If traveling with these, I suggest you use the E.Z. Foil Ready Mix Cake Pans (12¼ x 8¼ x 1¼ inches), and do not cut brownies until ready to serve.

Graham Cracker Pralines

If you have a real sweet tooth, these are for you.

Preheat oven to 350°.

Melt butter and brown sugar and mix well.

Place crackers in a greased jelly-roll pan. Spread melted butter and sugar over crackers. Sprinkle with chopped nuts.

Bake for 18 minutes. Cool and cut into desired size.

YIELD: 35 TO 42 COOKIES

½ pound butter
1 cup brown sugar
   cinnamon or plain graham crackers
1½ cups chopped nuts

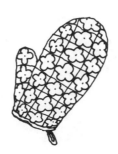

Miniature Cream Puffs

These always meet with acclaim. Make the puffs large or small; when ready to serve, fill with the chocolate mousse or lemon filling, and top with whipped cream.

1	cup boiling water
¼	pound butter
1	cup sifted flour
⅓	teaspoon salt
4	eggs

Preheat oven to 450°.

Add the butter to the boiling water. Stir with a wooden spoon until butter melts. Add flour and salt all at once. Stir the mixture vigorously.

Cook, stirring constantly, until the dough pulls away from the sides of the pan and forms a ball around the spoon.

Remove from heat and cool slightly.

Add the eggs, one at a time, beating smoothly after each.

For large puffs, drop by heaping tablespoonfuls about 3 inches apart on a parchment-covered baking sheet. Bake for 15 minutes. Reduce heat to 325° and bake for an additional 25 minutes.

For miniature puffs, drop by a scant tablespoon about 2 inches apart on a parchment-covered baking sheet. Bake as above, but reduce the baking time. Watch carefully. Cool on wire rack.

When ready to serve, cut off tops and crisp up tops and bottoms in a 350° oven for just a few minutes. Fill and serve.

YIELD: 24 MINIATURE PUFFS OR 12 LARGE PUFFS

Chocolate Mousse

This will delight all chocolate lovers, whether served alone or as a filling for cream puffs. Remember, when whipping cream, always have the bowl and the beaters ice cold. Do not use a food processor; use your electric mixer.

Beat cream until stiff. Add melted chocolate, egg yolks, orange rind, and liqueur and blend well. Set aside.

Beat egg whites with sugar into a stiff meringue. Fold into cream mixture.

Remove from refrigerator at least 30 minutes before spooning into cream puffs or serving alone.

YIELD: ENOUGH FOR 24 MINIATURE PUFFS

1	pint whipping cream
12	ounces semisweet chocolate, melted
2	eggs, at room temperature, separated
½	cup sugar
1	teaspoon orange rind
⅓	cup orange-chocolate liqueur or any liqueur of your choice that blends well with chocolate

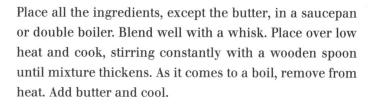

Lemon Filling

3	large eggs
¾	cup sugar
⅓	cup fresh lemon juice
3	teaspoons grated fresh lemon rind
6	tablespoons butter, room temperature

Place all the ingredients, except the butter, in a saucepan or double boiler. Blend well with a whisk. Place over low heat and cook, stirring constantly with a wooden spoon until mixture thickens. As it comes to a boil, remove from heat. Add butter and cool.

Refrigerate for several hours so that filling becomes firm and flavors blend. May be refrigerated overnight.

Spoon into cream puffs when ready to serve.

YIELD: ENOUGH TO FILL 24 MINIATURE PUFFS

Doralee's Triple-Threat Delights

I developed this recipe several years ago, after tasting something similar at a private club. They would not divulge their recipe, so I decided to try to see what I could do. I came pretty close. This is very rich, but very delicious!

Preheat oven to 350°.

For the dough, place butter or margarine and flour in a food processor. Blend with the steel knife until crumbly. Add remaining ingredients and process until well blended. Remove from processor and knead into a ball. You can either roll this out to fit a greased 11½ x 16½-inch baking pan, or press it into the pan. Bake for 10 to 15 minutes (it will be firm around the edges).

For the filling, beat the eggs slightly and combine well with the remaining ingredients. Remove dough from oven and pour the filling over the hot crust. Spread evenly to distribute nuts.

Return to 350° oven and bake for 25 to 30 minutes, or until filling is firm around the edges and just slightly firm in the center. Cool very well before cutting. Cut into narrow bars.

YIELD: AT LEAST 48 PIECES

COOKIE DOUGH

- ½ pound butter or margarine
- 2½ cups flour
- ½ cup sugar
- 1 extra large egg
- 1 teaspoon vanilla extract

FILLING

- 4 eggs
- 1½ cups light or dark Karo syrup
- 1½ cups sugar
- 3 tablespoons butter or margarine
- 1½ teaspoons vanilla extract
- 1 cup coarsely chopped pecans
- 1 cup coarsely chopped blanched almonds
- 1 cup coarsely chopped walnuts

Rugelach

Rugelach, a sour-cream or cream-cheese pastry, has been presented in many forms as it has come down through the generations. Rugelach can be small, be chunky, filled with fruit, and now even with chocolate chips. While there are many different types of pastry, fillings, and shapes, the following are my versions of rugelach.

DOUGH

2½ cups flour
½   pound butter
12 ounces cream cheese

EGG WASH

Beat one egg until frothy
with ⅛ cup water

TOPPING

cinnamon and sugar

Place the dough ingredients in the food processor and blend very well. Form dough into a ball and place in refrigerator overnight.

Combine ingredients for one of the fillings.

Preheat oven to 350°.

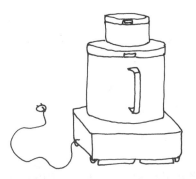

Roll dough into ¼-inch-thick circles—the size depends on the size of the rugelach desired. The larger the circle, the larger the piece will be. Spread with fillings. With a pizza cutter, cut circle into wedges resembling a pinwheel. Roll up each wedge from the outside into the center, curving it into a crescent. Place on parchment-covered cookie sheets, brush with egg wash, and sprinkle with cinnamon and sugar. Bake for 20 to 25 minutes, or until golden brown.

YIELD: 24 TO 48 RUGELACH

FILLING NO. 1

3½ ounces dried sour cherries or cranberries, finely chopped

½ cup sugar

1 cup toasted chopped walnuts

¼ pound sweet butter, melted

2 teaspoons cinnamon

1 teaspoon allspice

⅛ teaspoon salt

FILLING NO. 2

1 cup plum or raspberry preserves

½ cup chopped walnuts

½ cup golden raisins

juice of ½ lemon

1 tablespoon ground cinnamon

4 tablespoons butter, melted

Chocolate-Kahlúa Pecan Tart

Pecan pie has always been one of my favorites. This is "kicked up" a bit by using a little Kahlúa and some bittersweet chocolate.

TART PASTRY

1	cup flour
⅓	cup powdered sugar
12	tablespoons butter
⅛	teaspoon salt

FILLING

8	ounces Baker's bitter-sweet chocolate, chopped into small chunks
4	eggs, slightly beaten
¾	cup dark corn syrup
¼	cup Kahlúa
¾	cup brown sugar
3	tablespoons butter, melted
2	teaspoons vanilla extract
⅛	teaspoon salt
2	cups pecan halves

Preheat oven to 350°.

Blend pastry ingredients in food processor and press into an 8- or 9-inch tart pan.

Sprinkle the chocolate chunks on the bottom of the unbaked tart shell. Mix eggs, corn syrup, Kahlúa, sugar, butter, and vanilla until well blended. Pour in half of the filling. Arrange the pecans over the filling. Pour in balance of filling.

Bake for 50 to 60 minutes, or until knife inserted halfway between center and edge comes out clean.

Cool completely before removing outer rim from tart pan. If using this for a dessert table, pre-cut the pieces, but serve the tart whole. Serve with whipped cream.

YIELD: 8 TO 10 SERVINGS

Turtle Pecan Cheesecake

This fabulous little number was given to me by a lovely lady, Kathleen. Please don't count the calories—just enjoy!

Preheat oven to 450°.

Combine the crushed chocolate wafers with the melted butter and press into a greased 9-inch springform pan.

For the filling, beat the cream cheese until fluffy. Add the sugar, flour, salt, and vanilla and blend. Add the eggs, one at a time, and blend well. Add the whipping cream. Blend well and pour over the crust. Bake for 10 minutes. Reduce heat to 200° and continue baking for 35 to 40 minutes, until set to the touch. Remove and cool on rack.

For the toppings, combine caramels and cream. Stir over low heat until smooth. Drizzle over the cheesecake.

Combine chocolate, butter, and cream. Stir over low heat until smooth. Drizzle over the caramel topping.

Top with toasted pecans.

YIELD: 12 SERVINGS

CRUST
- 2 cups crushed chocolate ice cream wafers
- 4 tablespoons butter, melted

FILLING
- 20 ounces cream cheese, softened
- 1 cup sugar
- 1½ tablespoons flour
- ¼ teaspoon salt
- 1 teaspoon vanilla extract
- 3 whole eggs
- 2 tablespoons whipping cream

CARAMEL TOPPING
- 14 ounces of caramels
- ⅓ cup whipping cream

CHOCOLATE TOPPING
- 4 ounces German sweet chocolate
- 1 teaspoon butter
- 2 tablespoons whipping cream

Cognac Brownies

These are sinfully rich, and can be served in small pieces or "plated" as the main dessert. If a stronger liqueur flavor is desired, by all means, go for it.

¼	pound plus 2 table-spoons butter
3	tablespoons peanut oil
5	ounces unsweetened baking chocolate
2⅛	cups brown sugar
4	eggs
6	tablespoons of a good cognac liqueur
3½	tablespoons Droste's cocoa
1¼	cups flour
¼	teaspoon salt
½	teaspoon cinnamon

Preheat oven to 350°.

In a large Pyrex container, melt the butter, oil, and chocolate in the microwave oven for 7 minutes at 30 percent power. Remove and stir until smooth. Add the brown sugar and blend well. Add the eggs, one at a time, mixing well. Sift the cocoa, flour, salt, and cinnamon together and add to the chocolate mixture.

Grease and lightly flour a 9-inch square pan. Pour batter into pan and smooth evenly. Bake for 20 to 30 minutes. Remove from oven, cool for about 10 minutes, and invert onto a cake rack placed on a large sheet of heavy-duty aluminum foil. While cake is cooling, prepare the glaze.

Heat all ingredients in a microwaveable dish at 30 percent power for 6 to 7 minutes. Remove and mix until smooth. Spoon generously over cake and allow to cool for several hours so topping will set. The balance of the topping can be stored in a glass jar in the refrigerator.

Cut into small squares and place in miniature papers, or serve as a dessert by dribbling raspberry sauce (see p. 79) on a dessert plate and placing large squares on the plate with a few fresh raspberries.

YIELD: AT LEAST 48 SMALL PIECES OR 9 LARGE PIECES

GLAZE

1¼ cups semisweet chocolate chips

½ cup peanut or corn oil

2 to 3 tablespoons cognac (to taste)

Marsha's Trifle

The very first time I tasted a trifle, my aunt Selma was visiting us from Capetown, South Africa. We were having a party in her honor and she insisted on preparing a "trifle." My daughter Marsha has made trifles throughout the years and they were scrumptious. This is her version.

The quantities of the ingredients will vary depending upon the size of the crystal bowl or brandy snifter used. I will tell you how my daughter arranged the ingredients, and the rest is up to you. Believe me, it is very easy, and nothing is more delicious!

1	or more of very rich pound cake
	raspberry or strawberry preserves
2	10- to 12-ounce packages of frozen raspberries or strawberries (in juice)
	sliced bananas
	rum
2	packages of a very rich vanilla pudding prepared according to instructions on package
	toasted sliced almonds
	whipped cream

Cut the pound cake into slices about ½-inch thick. Spread each slice generously with the raspberry or strawberry preserves. Drizzle about 2 teaspoons of rum on each slice of cake.

Arrange a layer of pound cake in the bottom of the bowl you will be using. You will probably have to cut the slices of cake to make them fit. Cover with a layer of sliced bananas, some of the frozen berries, a thick layer of vanilla pudding, and some of the sliced almonds. Repeat the procedure. You will see a ribbon effect. Drizzle a little more rum over the top, and be sure you finish with a layer of toasted almonds.

Cover with plastic wrap and refrigerate for at least 6 to 8 hours. When ready to serve, top with some whipped cream.

YIELD: SHOULD BE AT LEAST 10 TO 12 SERVINGS

Brunch

Brunch

I must admit that brunch has always been a favorite of mine, whether at home or at a restaurant. The only drawback is that one must rise early in the day if brunch is held at home. I hope you'll be inventive, but here are a few suggestions.

Bear in mind that I always purchase bagels and have them sliced at the bakery.

Naturally, the type of cream cheese is your choice. You can either make your own lox (recipe in *Grandma Doralee Patinkin's Jewish Family Cookbook*), or purchase the type of lox you prefer.

I like to arrange the lox with capers and sliced sweet onions, decorated with lots of parsley.

Brunch

Lox, Bagels, and Cream Cheese
with Capers and Sweet Onions

Fruit Shrub

Broiled Grapefruit

Brunch Soufflé

Chicken Salad Laurie

Curried Rice Salad

Cinnamon-Applesauce Noodle Kugel

Waldorf Salad Mold

Cucumbers, Tomatoes, and Artichoke Hearts

Mini Orange Muffins

Imperial Pound Cake
and/or
selections from Sweet Table chapter

Fruit Shrub

This is always a winner at our brunches or luncheons. If you're going to use gin or vodka, be careful. I speak from experience!

Place the washed green leaves in the bottom of a ring mold. Fill with a little water and freeze. Arrange the cherries as you wish in the next layer, fill with a little water, and freeze. When frozen, fill the mold with water to the top and store in the freezer.

When you are ready to serve the shrub, combine the ginger ale, club soda, and orange juice in a punch bowl. Add the orange sherbet and blend. Shrub should be thick. Add gin or vodka if you wish.

You can always adjust the amounts according to your needs. Remove the ice from the mold and place in the punch bowl.

YIELD: 12 TO 16 SERVINGS

1	quart ginger ale
1	quart club soda
1	quart orange juice
1	quart orange sherbet
1	cup gin or vodka (optional)
	small green leaves
	maraschino cherries

Broiled Grapefruit

When grapefruits are in season, I love to serve them, either whole or in sections. I use half a grapefruit or ¾ cup grapefruit sections per person.

grapefruits, cut in half or sectioned

maraschino cherries, with juice

ground cloves or nutmeg

Prepare grapefruits or sections for serving and place in a baking pan. Sprinkle with a little of the maraschino cherry juice and a sprinkle of ground cloves or nutmeg, whichever you prefer. Place a maraschino cherry in the center of the whole fruit or throw some cherries in with the segments.

Place under the broiler and heat for a minute or two.

To serve, place the halves of the fruit in small bowls; place the segments with a cherry or two in pretty glass dessert dishes.

Brunch Soufflé

This soufflé has been around for as many years as I can remember. It is wonderful. You can reduce the fat content by substituting the items shown in parentheses.

Preheat oven to 325°.

Mix eggs, milk, mustard, salt, pepper, and curry powder together. Grease an oven-to-table casserole (8½ x 11 inches) and layer the bread in the casserole, covering each layer with cheese and some of the egg mixture. Top with the cheese. Refrigerate overnight.

Bake for 1 hour, or until golden brown.

YIELD: 8 TO 10 SERVINGS

3	whole eggs (or ¾ cup egg substitute)
2	cups low-fat milk (or skim)
1	teaspoon Dijon mustard
1	teaspoon salt
½	teaspoon white pepper
½	teaspoon curry powder
8	slices white bread, crusts removed, spread with butter (or margarine) and cut into squares
8	ounces shredded mild or sharp Cheddar cheese (or low or nonfat)

Chicken Salad Laurie

When my granddaughter Laurie was a little girl, this was the way she liked her chicken salad. The chutney makes the difference.

2 to 3 cups cubed cooked breast of chicken	Combine the chicken, celery, nuts, salt, and pepper.
1 cup diced celery	Process the chutney until it's semismooth.
½ cup coarsely chopped toasted pecans	Dissolve the curry powder in the mayonnaise, then add the chutney to it. Add mayonnaise mixture to the chicken mixture.
1 teaspoon salt	
⅛ teaspoon white pepper	
¼ cup mango chutney	Blend and chill. Adjust seasonings. If you like a very moist salad, add more dressing or chutney, or both.
1 teaspoon curry powder	
½ cup mayonnaise	YIELD: 4 TO 6 SERVINGS

Curried Rice Salad

This is a great summer salad and also an excellent item for a brunch buffet.

Combine all the ingredients and toss well. Cover and chill.

YIELD: 4 TO 6 SERVINGS

1	cup cooked long-grain rice
½	cup chopped celery
¼	cup finely chopped green onions
¼	cup chopped red bell pepper
½	cup toasted slivered almonds
¼	cup red wine vinaigrette dressing
¼	cup fresh lemon juice
1	teaspoon curry powder
	salt and pepper to taste

Cinnamon-Applesauce Noodle Kugel

Another wonderful kugel that can be made with fat and sugar or without. The optional substitutions are shown in parentheses. I have made this for several very large parties at our temple, and it has always met with great success.

4	tablespoons butter (or corn oil margarine) melted
2	eggs, slightly beaten (or ½ cup egg substitute)
1	cup sour cream (can use light or fat-free)
2	cups cinnamon applesauce
1	scant teaspoon cinnamon
¼	cup sugar (or 1 teaspoon Sweet 'n Low)
1½	teaspoons salt
1	cup raisins (optional)
1	8-ounce package semi-broad noodles, cooked according to instructions on package, drained, and rinsed with cold water
1½	cups cinnamon graham crackers, crushed
	dots of butter

Preheat oven to 350°.

Combine all the ingredients—except crushed cinnamon graham crackers and butter—and place in a greased oven-proof casserole (approximately 13 x 9 inches).

Top with crushed cinnamon graham crackers and dot with butter.

Bake for 1 hour. When done it will have a nice, crunchy appearance.

YIELD: 12 SERVINGS

Waldorf Salad Mold

This has always been one of my favorites. It is great with a brunch buffet, but is wonderful with poultry, meat, or even with sandwiches.

Dissolve gelatin in hot water. Add cold fruit cocktail liquid. Allow to cool for 30 minutes.

Add the fruit cocktail to the cooled gelatin and then add the celery, nuts, and apples.

Pour into a greased ring mold and chill until firm. Unmold, garnish with lemon leaves and your favorite fruit in the center, and serve.

YIELD: 4 TO 6 SERVINGS

1	3-ounce package lime gelatin
1	cup boiling water
1	cup cold fruit cocktail juice. Even it out with cold water.
1	1-pound can fruit cocktail, drained
1	cup diced celery
½	cup chopped toasted walnuts
1	large Granny Smith apple, chopped

Cucumbers, Tomatoes, and Artichoke Hearts

A refreshing complement to any brunch or luncheon menu. It's the touch of seasoned rice vinegar that makes the difference.

sliced beefsteak tomatoes

sliced English cucumbers, scrubbed but unpeeled

marinated artichoke hearts

fresh parsley sprigs

seasoned rice vinegar

Slice the tomatoes and cucumbers with a serrated knife. Arrange the tomato slices, cucumber slices, and drained artichoke hearts on a serving platter, using the sprigs of parsley for a garnish. Drizzle with the seasoned rice vinegar.

Use a serrated slicer

Mini Orange Muffins

I just love to make these little muffins. They're great for a brunch or luncheon, or just for a quick breakfast. This recipe can also be made into two mini loaves.

Preheat oven to 375° for muffins, 350° for a loaf.

Dissolve baking soda in the buttermilk.

Cream the butter and sugar. Add the eggs and blend until light and fluffy. Add the buttermilk, flour, salt, and grated rind and blend well. Pour into miniature muffin tins and bake for 15 minutes.

Meanwhile, combine sugar and orange juice and cook over low heat until sugar dissolves. When muffins are done, dip each muffin in the sauce and place on a cake rack to cool.

If making loaves, bake for 30 to 45 minutes. When done, pour sauce over loaves and cool.

YIELD: 36 TO 48 MINI MUFFINS, 6 TO 8 SLICES PER LOAF.

1	teaspoon baking soda
1	cup buttermilk
¼	pound butter
1	cup sugar
2	eggs
2	cups flour
¼	teaspoon salt
	grated rind of 2 oranges (save juice for sauce)

SAUCE

1	cup brown sugar
	juice of 1 orange

Imperial Pound Cake

This was a favorite of "The Fraternity" from the kitchen of my dear friend, Shirley Krieberg.

1	pound Imperial margarine
2	cups powdered sugar
6	whole eggs
2	teaspoons vanilla extract or lemon juice and rind of an orange
3	cups sifted cake flour
½	teaspoon salt

Preheat oven to 350°.

Combine margarine and sugar and mix well. Add the eggs, one at a time, beating well after each. Add the vanilla or lemon juice and orange rind.

Sift the cake flour and the salt together and add to butter and egg mixture. Blend, but do not overbeat.

Turn into a greased and lightly floured large loaf pan–16 x 5 x 4 inches deep. Bake for 75 to 90 minutes. Test before removing from oven.

YIELD: 8 TO 12 SERVINGS

Patio Supper/
Barbecue

Patio Supper/Barbecue

Living in the Southwest has given me the opportunity to entertain on my patio quite often.

However, when we lived in the Midwest, almost every Sunday during the warm weather we would have at least twenty people for supper. Hot dogs and hamburgers were always popular, especially when the children were young, but we always managed to please the adults as well with something a little more grown up. When you serve outdoors, try to keep it simple.

Avail yourself of all the attractive party goods, both plastic and paper, on the market, and above all have fun with your guests.

Patio Supper/Barbecue

Baked Brie
Chicken Wing Drumettes
Mushroom Tartlets
Cocktail Franks

Barbecued Tri-Tip Steak
and/or
Oven-Barbecued Beef Ribs

Honey Mustard-Apricot Chicken

Apricot-Rice Dish
and/or
Linguine with Mushrooms and Sun-Dried Tomatoes

Caesar Salad

Lemon (or Lime) Delight

Baked Brie

While we now limit our cheese consumption considerably, I still love to serve cheeses for a party. I must say, they do not last long. There are many ways to bake a round of Brie. This is one of the most delicious and one of the easiest to prepare.

Preheat oven to 500°.

Place the round of Brie on a baking pan, removing the top rind but leaving a narrow rim all around. Combine the preserves, liqueur, and brown sugar. Frost the brie with preserves mixture and bake for 4 to 5 minutes. Immediately sprinkle with the toasted sliced almonds and remove with a large spatula to a serving platter and allow the preserves to drip down the sides. Serve with a mixture of small crackers.

YIELD: 8 TO 10 SERVINGS

1	*8-inch round of Brie*
½	*cup raspberry preserves*
1	*tablespoon Grand Marnier liqueur*
1	*tablespoon brown sugar*
2 to 3	*tablespoons toasted sliced almonds*

Chicken Wing Drumettes

Loved by the kids as well as the adults, these do well for an entrée as well as an appetizer. You can use my marinade or try a Thai peanut sauce available at any supermarket.

24 chicken wing
   drumettes

1 teaspoon minced
  fresh ginger

3 cloves minced garlic

MARINADE

½ cup soy sauce

½ cup apricot preserves

Preheat oven to 375°.

Spray a large baking pan with vegetable spray. Arrange the drumettes in the pan. Combine the balance of the ingredients and cover the drumettes generously with the marinade.

Bake for 1 hour, basting often. Be sure the drumettes are not pink at the bone. When done, they should be nicely glazed.

These can be made in advance and reheated either in the oven or the microwave.

YIELD: ALLOW 3 TO 4 PER PERSON

Mushroom Tartlets

These will melt in your mouth. I never have enough!

If using a pastry dough or sliced bread, roll the dough or the bread flat and use a 2½-inch cutter to make the rounds. The pastry dough or the bread rounds should be fitted into well-greased mini muffin tins (2½ inches). The butterflake rolls and English muffins should be slightly toasted before spreading.

For the filling, melt the butter in a large frying pan. Add the shallots and mushrooms and sauté until the liquid has disappeared. Add the egg yolk and seasonings and stir well. Add the cream cheese and continue to stir until well blended. Add the dissolved cornstarch and bring to a boil.

Stir until mixture thickens. Remove from heat. Place in refrigerator until ready to use.

Preheat oven to 400°. Fill muffin cups, sprinkle with paprika, and bake for 15 to 30 minutes; or spread muffins or rolls, sprinkle with paprika, and broil until hot and bubbly.

YIELD: 24 TO 36 PIECES

TARTLET SHELLS
pastry dough

rounds from white sliced bread

butterflake rolls, separated or English muffins, cut into fourths

FILLING
4	*tablespoons butter*
2	*shallots, chopped*
1	*pound chopped mushrooms*
1	*egg yolk*
½	*teaspoon garlic powder*
¼	*teaspoon salt*
⅛	*teaspoon pepper*
¼	*teaspoon curry powder*
4	*ounces cream cheese*
2	*tablespoons cornstarch dissolved in ¼ cup cold water*

Cocktail Franks

As far as I am concerned, hot dogs in any form are the ultimate in "fun food." These are always a hit with the kids as well as their parents. After all, we don't serve them every day!

36	cocktail frankfurters
½	cup chili sauce
½	cup French's yellow mustard
½	cup grape jam
1½	tablespoons fresh lemon juice

Put all ingredients in a large pot. Bring to boil, and allow to simmer for at least an hour.

Transfer to a chafing dish. Serve with toothpicks.

YIELD: 6 TO 8 SERVINGS

Barbecued Tri-Tip Steak

Tri-tip is a wonderfully flavorful but not always so tender piece of meat. It must be marinated for several hours to tenderize. Grill whole pieces and then cut into serving-size strips. This cut grills very fast. All grills cook differently, so test a small amount to insure the correct cooking time.

To make the marinade, combine soy sauce, olive oil, and Worcestershire sauce.

Before marinating the steak, pierce the meat several times. This will allow the sauce to penetrate. Turn and brush with marinade frequently.

When ready, place the meat on the grill. Combine any remaining marinade with ¼ cup barbecue sauce and brush the meat while grilling.

YIELD: 6 TO 8 SERVINGS

4	pounds tri-tip steak
½	cup soy sauce
2	tablespoons olive oil
¼	cup Worcestershire sauce
¼	cup barbecue sauce

Oven-Barbecued Beef Ribs

An indulgence to be frowned upon, but I love them. Nothing is messier to eat, but they're great at a party. I figure at least three ribs per person.

¾	cup brown sugar
½	cup ketchup
½	cup soy sauce
2	tablespoons hoisin sauce
1	teaspoon black pepper
1	cup chicken stock
2	racks of beef ribs, separated
	garlic powder

Combine everything except the ribs and garlic powder and blend well. Season the ribs well with the garlic powder. Pour three quarters of the sauce over the ribs and marinate for at least 8 hours, brushing occasionally.

When ready, preheat oven to 350°. Place ribs on a rack in a roasting pan and pour in 1 cup of water to prevent smoking. After 45 minutes turn and baste with sauce. Return to oven and roast for another 30 minutes. Remove ribs from rack, empty the pan of water and fat, and place the ribs in the pan. Brush with the balance of the sauce. Reduce heat to 325°, cover with aluminum foil, and continue to roast for 45 minutes, or until done.

YIELD: 6 SERVINGS

Honey Mustard—Apricot Chicken

A quick and delicious way to serve that skinless, boneless breast. These can also be made on the grill.

Blend the mustard, preserves, and ginger. Spread on the chicken breasts and broil for 8 minutes on each side, brushing well with the sauce.

YIELD: 4 SERVINGS

⅓ cup honey mustard

3 to 4 tablespoons puréed apricot preserves

1 teaspoon ground ginger

4 skinless, boneless breasts of chicken

Apricot-Rice Dish

This is a great complement to chicken, beef, or lamb.

1	cup chopped dried apricots
1	cup chopped sweet onion
1	cup chopped celery
4	tablespoons butter
3	cups cooked long-grain rice (I never use instant rice)
¼	teaspoon turmeric
½	teaspoon cinnamon
¼	teaspoon nutmeg
½	teaspoon curry powder
¼	teaspoon salt
⅛	teaspoon pepper

Sauté the apricots, onion, and celery in the butter. Add to the cooked rice and add all the seasonings. Transfer to an ovenproof casserole and reheat in microwave just before serving.

YIELD: 8 TO 10 SERVINGS

Linguine with Mushrooms and Sun-Dried Tomatoes

My three favorite ingredients plus lots of garlic. How bad can it be?

In a deep frying pan, heat the olive oil. Sauté the garlic for about 5 minutes. Add the broth, tomatoes, and red pepper. Cook for about 3 more minutes.

When ready to serve, add the cooked linquine and toss until desired tenderness. Sprinkle with cheese, and serve at once.

YIELD: 3 TO 4 SERVINGS

3	tablespoons olive oil
4	garlic cloves, crushed (the more the better)
½	cup chicken or clear vegetable broth
½	cup chopped sun-dried tomatoes (without oil)
¼	teaspoon minced red pepper
½	pound linguine pasta (prepared al dente)
	your favorite grated Italian cheese

Caesar Salad

There is no doubt that Caesar is the most popular salad served today. Just remember to keep the romaine dry so that the dressing will adhere. You can, of course, invent your own luncheon Caesar by serving with strips of grilled chicken, salmon, or whatever moves you.

juice of 1 lemon

2 *teaspoons red wine vinegar*

1 *tablespoon anchovy paste*

2 *large garlic cloves, crushed*

⅓ *cup extra-virgin olive oil*

2 *egg whites, slightly beaten*

⅓ *cup fine Parmesan cheese (or a blend of Parmesan and Romano)*

freshly ground pepper to taste

2 *pounds romaine hearts, torn into bit size pieces*

croutons (see note)

Combine the lemon juice, vinegar, anchovy paste, and crushed garlic and blend well. Slowly whisk in the olive oil and blend. Add the slightly beaten egg whites and the Parmesan cheese and blend well. When ready to serve, toss over the romaine hearts and top with some additional cheese and croutons, if desired.

YIELD: 4 TO 6 SIDE SALADS, OR 2 LARGE LUNCHEON SALADS

Note 🌹 Cut several slices of a country-style bread into small chunks. Sauté the bread chunks in olive oil and season lightly with salt; or bake in a 450° oven for about 6 minutes, until golden brown.

Lemon (or Lime) Delight

Arlene Goldberg was right, this is yummy in the tummy. Try this for Passover, substituting Passover mandelbrot crumbs for the graham cracker crumbs.

Preheat oven to 350°.

Combine all the crust ingredients. Line a 9-inch springform pan with the mixture. Bake for 5 minutes and remove from oven.

Mix the gelatin with the cold water. Set aside.

Beat the egg yolks until thick. Add juice and zest. Cook the egg mixture with 1 cup of the sugar until thick. Cool.

Liquefy the gelatin by placing it over hot water or in the microwave oven for 2 to 3 seconds. Add to the yolk mixture and blend well.

Beat the egg whites with the remaining ¼ cup of sugar into stiff peaks. Fold the yolk mixture into the beaten egg whites.

Pour into baked crust. Cover with plastic wrap and freeze overnight or longer. Remove from freezer about 1 hour before serving.

YIELD: 8 TO 10 SERVINGS

CRUST

1	cup graham cracker crumbs
½	cup sugar
8	tablespoons butter, melted
1	teaspoon ground cinnamon
1	cup toasted chopped pecans

FILLING

1	tablespoon (1 envelope) unflavored gelatin
¼	cup cold water
7	eggs, separated
3	lemons, juice and grated zest
1¼	cups sugar

Index